Things Your Mother Never Told You About Love

Things Your Mother Never Told You About Love

Juhi Pande

EBURY PRESS

An imprint of Penguin Random House

EBURY PRESS

USA | Canada | UK | Ireland | Australia
New Zealand | India | South Africa | China | Singapore

Ebury Press is part of the Penguin Random House group of companies
whose addresses can be found at global.penguinrandomhouse.com

Published by Penguin Random House India Pvt. Ltd
4th Floor, Capital Tower 1, MG Road,
Gurugram 122 002, Haryana, India

Penguin
Random House
India

Published by Random House India in 2014
Published in Ebury Press by Penguin Random House India 2023

10 9 8 7 6 5 4 3 2

ISBN 9788184004380

Typeset in Sabon by R. Ajith Kumar

Printed at Repro India Limited

www.penguin.co.in

FSC
www.fsc.org
MIX
Paper from
responsible sources
FSC® C047271

This is a legitimate digitally printed version of the book and therefore might not have certain extra finishing on the cover.

I dedicate this book to 1997

Contents

1

Chaos

'WE ACCEPT THE LOVE WE THINK WE DESERVE.'

Stephen Chbosky wrote in *The Perks of Being a Wallflower*. Well, to him I want to say, 'Damn you, Stephen Chbosky! Who do you think you are with that unpronounceable last name and the ability to frame a sentence that made me weep?!'

We all know that girls love boys love girls, and they turn into women who love men who love women. And no matter how much one would like to clutter their life with work or distract themselves with friends or treks or travels, at the end of the day it is the matters of the heart that take control of our deeper senses.

In my opinion, there are few people who have managed to find that one person who they want to spend their eternity with. For the rest of us it is a matter of:

a) Trial and error

b) Making do

c) Keep on looking and lucking out

d) Cats and a rocking chair

If you think about it, all the options seem pretty optimistic except for b.

Unless of course you are allergic to cats and/or rocking chairs, in which case d is a pretty bad idea too.

We live in a time when people are quite comfortable discussing their relationships with others, be it specific to a tiny tiff or the general workings of their tumultuous or flawed partnership. We also live in a time where the number of people meeting their shrinks for 'stress' (which is usually brought on by their relationship problems) is on the rise, and 'going to my therapist' is becoming as hipster as going for an obsure Indie band secret concert.

But my point is that, when it becomes okay to share the status of your complicated relationship with 900 of your friends on a social networking site, we can safely say that our definition of private/personal is bent out of shape. When people start flaunting their flawed relationships like a cool scar, it makes me wonder why they're in it in the first place.

We could be very basic in our approach to love. If you like someone, you should choose to be with him or her. And if it doesn't work out then you can call it quits and move on. Clearly, I should have been a philosopher.

But we all know that life and love are not black and white. Women and men are terribly different animals.

Therefore, in a world willing to tear its sternum open and show its heart to everybody, things get even more complicated.

The generations before us (our parents) believed in stoicism. They were in it to win it. Most times, two people got together, willingly or forced by their parents, gagged/bound, and they made it a point to try and work their best at keeping the marriage or relationship together. People didn't wash their dirty laundry in the open, you didn't meet a stranger on a train ride who emptied their emotional baggage onto you, and friends didn't constantly whine about their other halves.

People tried.

Don't get me wrong. I don't think we don't try. I feel that we attempt trying in front of large audiences comprising friends, family, and sundry passersby. We have morphed into a species that needs its own personal amphitheater and a round of applause on cue. Subtlety and handling our problems on our own is but a distant idea, mostly dismissed at first thought.

Which brings me to the question: is that such a bad thing? Is it bad that we live in a state of flux? If change is the only constant, then this ebb and flow should work beautifully in our current state of affairs. Should we wear our lament on our sleeve and make it the last conversation that ends the night? The last thought we think of be of the person we are in love with, who may or may not love us back? Aren't there bigger things to think of? Isn't the Indian Supreme Court going back to the dark ages by calling gay sex illegal? Isn't the ice age coming? What is the capital of North Korea?

I think it's just a new way of adjusting to life. Social evolution. A paradigm shift in dealing with our emotions. And because it is all so new, everyone is running around asking each other questions for which no one has answers. 'Here! This is my problem, solve it', gets an answer of 'Okay. Sure. But first, listen to my problem, it is more important'. It makes no sense. Nothing really gets solved and we walk around in a maze full of noise and opinions. Most of which aren't even our own.

Men and women deal with problems differently. And most of the times choose a partner who seems great on paper, and fits the idea of the perfect person. But sometimes, that's just an idea that has been drilled into their cranium by magazines, peers, and a warped sense of perfection.

I also feel that a woman's ability to discern a good thing from a bad is akin to an octopus learning how to break dance. This is the worst analogy in the world because it makes no sense, but I'm sure you get what I'm saying.

Most smart women tend to make a beeline for the bad guys because of everything that their veneer promises. The good guys with their niceness and eager-to-please sensitive attitudes end up finishing last or sometimes are not even asked to be a part of the race. The ruggedness, the dismissiveness, the nonchalance and the hard to get demeanor of the bad boys, all make a façade that seems irresistible. And it's not like the bad guys are gangsters who wear fedoras and do nefarious things. These are just your regular, below average sort of bad guys who can't spell or treat a woman right. Therefore, you have women whining and men cribbing. I'm not going to focus on the men cribbing because frankly I can't get into their heads. What I can do is deconstruct the women and try and figure out a way to have a quick and easy solution to this problem. Right after which I will solve the energy crisis and save the world from hunger.

Seriously though, let's get down to brass tacks. Boys break our brains. We think we know them, but we don't. We think we know what we want, but we don't. Use the last two sentences in an equation and you have yourself a Rubik's cube from hell.

We have to rely on 'good sense prevailing', which is NEVER the case, or as I mentioned earlier, we have to go through our own trial and error. Which of course leads to heartbreak, because let's face it, how many people do you know who've ended up with their first love? The list usually stops at Cinderella.

And maybe that's not such a bad thing. Life happens to us. We ride that wave and in some time realize exactly what it is we want thereby making the aforementioned problem that much simpler. Of course, there will be anomalies. There will be people who never learn from their mistakes or realize what they want. And we may have been these people too, a while back, with a certain relationship, but later than sooner we understand what is good for us. For the few who don't, they're called Rihanna.

With age comes wisdom...and fatigue. Patience seems to run out faster, giving enough space for logic. And logic is all you need, right after love. And yes, they do go hand in hand. As a woman in the 21st century, having been in a few relationships I think I can safely say I know what I want in a man. Better still, I know exactly what I *don't* want in a man. I feel I can't be the only woman saying this, because, I may be special and all, but I don't have a stretch limo and diamond studded grills, so I can't be that special. For all the other women who feel the same way, this book is not for you. But if you've already bought it, keep reading because you get a free puppy once you hit page 150.

This is for all the girls who haven't yet unraveled

themselves. Who still need to get to that 'aha!' moment in their lives where suddenly things make sense and logic climbs forward from the backseat and takes control of the wheel. This is for anyone who's felt stuck, who's had inertia take over their entire being, who's conflicted and not been sure if they're happy.

Black, white, and everything right.

That's what I'm going to try and do. Give you a bird's eye view of a few conceivable situations and lay it down for you in the simplest possible manner so you can hold that up and use it as a mirror.

Right after which I'll attach a few 'Shri Shris' as a prefix to my name.

2

The Best Phase of Boy–Girl Relationships

BHUJ HAS ALWAYS BEEN ARID. AND BETWEEN 1981 AND 1984 nothing changed. It remained arid. Not arid like how you imagine the word.

Much worse.

Much.

Everything would consistently have an even coating of dust the year round. It is possible that the term 'bone dry' got coined here. My mother tried to grow a hedge around our 'garden' of sand. The 'hedge' died, or rather it committed suicide in the first fortnight, and we were left with barbed wire. We had little choice but to be fine with it.

Our neighbours had a bougainvillea plant, and my friend Ruchira and I would pluck its flowers, squash them, and rub them on our hands. Let's just say Kyoto hadn't come up with Gameboy yet, so this was our only option for entertainment on hot afternoons. The evenings were better. We lived at an Air Force Base, which was sprinkled with kids my age. Everyone knew everyone. All the children went to the same school,

stepped out of their houses at 5 pm to play. I know I loved Ruchira, because if she didn't come out to play I would be heartbroken. And I'm sure I loved a few other people for similar reasons but I can't seem to remember their names.

What I do remember from that time is going to Mandvi beach with my parents, my father's friend sticking his toe in the sand and pulling out a tiny crab. I also remember going to Sunday Park in Ruchira's dad's car. This was the one patch of land in Bhuj where grass agreed to grow so people quickly built merry-go-rounds and swings in it. I remember my dad's Yezdi, I remember being stung by bees on my first day of school,

I remember my first school performance, I remember bike rides, hyenas laughing in the distance at night, I remember climbing the big slide in the playground and sliding down, expecting some sort of medal for making it back to terra ferma in once piece, I remember the heat, the sun. I don't remember fighting. I don't remember heartache. I don't remember hating boys, except for that kid who ate my hair. Maybe that's why I have that phase of my life saved away as pain free. Except for the odd knee scrape. The preciousness of it all. Or the idea of the preciousness of it all.

What I don't remember is being aware of boys. Or girls. They were just people who I hung out with for a few years before taking off to another place. Everyone did their thing, rode bikes, ran around, wore brown dungarees, and ate hair. The heartbreakers, soul shakers, lip smackers, sly winkers were yet to be born. The players, haters, lovers, clingers were but fledglings with no knowledge of their future avatars, which was hidden somewhere deep inside and would start to surface slowly like a blooming flower or an alien pod, opening up to reveal something that drips sulfuric acid.

This is the time when we live in the here and now, without being told to do so. It's akin to a constant state of meditation. Everything is in the moment, but not at all fleeting. If it were, it wouldn't stay with us forever. Our childhood, and everything we felt in it, would fade away, eventually. But it does not. Because it is so visceral. As is the love we feel. Which is why it manages to become the entire box of Best Phase of Boy–Girl Relationship.

There is such a thing.

No, really.

This is a time when we are borderline sentient, when we are the cutest we will ever be, and when eating mud is adorable. It's when we run around in our midget sizes with reckless abandon, with the wind in our hair and the sun in our face. It's when bawling with your uvula showing will get you more attention than less. But that aside, the innocence of the child is not something that anyone can overlook. There is no overbearing stress. Heck, there is no stress. The tiny human is completely dependent on its parent, who, in turn, deals with several levels of stress that seem to grow exponentially. The child on the other hand is one step short of golfing and sipping Martinis.

Making friends as children may take a little while, but once it happens, it forms a bond so strong and deep, that it stays with us forever. The sex of the other person never matters. Boys don't care about girls being boys, and girls don't care about boys being girls. Thinking is liberal enough to allow girls to play with guns and boys to play dress up without batting an eyelid. There's a lot of love, and sometimes hate, but it's pure, casual, and allowed to be taken for granted. All the cards are on the table. There are no aces up anyone's sleeve. The clarity of these relationships is sparkling. Freud said, 'Children are completely egoistic; they feel their needs intensely and strive ruthlessly to satisfy them.' Well, thank heavens they are young with underdeveloped non-adult brains because otherwise, by that theory, they would all be rabid wolves.

At this time needs are limited, basic, natural rather than nurturing. Hence the complications of a relationship (any sort of relationship) are missing. If you want to tear someone's hair off of their scalp and eat it, you can do it, because no one has handed you a life manual till then. If you are a boy and want to punch a girl as big or maybe even slightly bigger than you, you can. No one will hang you upside down and whip you for another ten years. Life is uncomplicated and everyone is equal. No one is playing anyone. Everyone is competing in 'who can leap the farthest' (and I'm mostly winning this), no one wears make-up, deception levels are sub zero, and you can wear a bear suit on a Tuesday afternoon and still have friends. It's great.

If someone could hit pause at this moment, things would be spectacular and humans wouldn't be the most hated species on the planet. At this age anything is possible. The ability to think up the absurd and believe in it without the help of psychotropic drugs is one of the highlights. Then, there's the ease of understanding everything in your own manner, with the help of your imagination. The list is endless and also a lot of fun. I remember when I was four, I used to have these dungarees, in brown, and every time I wore them, I would become insanely cool. I would develop an immediate swagger and feel a foot taller than all the other monkeys. I even have a photograph with one leg sticking out. (Cue Angelina Jolie!! This was 1984! I wore it first. You owe me money.) There was something about those dungarees. Or there was something about being four and invincible. That's the power of childhood. It allows you to turn a make-believe world in your head into a reality. (So, if my dungarees made me feel powerful and invincible, so be it.) And in that make-believe reality come friendships, first 'loves', 'boyfriends' and 'girlfriends'. We walk around professing our love for people and we mean it with a fearless honesty that we tend to squash in the coming years. But we don't carry the baggage of responsibility. Mostly because nothing is expected of us.

Our awareness is at a surface level at this point of time. Names are given to things. Rocks, books, hairbands, pink, mud, bicycle. We identify these things under categories and boys come under a category as well. Even though they seem the same as us, they are actually different and we realize that with bits and bobs of information such as them dressing differently, or the fact that they have different hair or don't like dolls (some of them do). Little girls form gangs and yell, 'Boys are stupid, throw rocks at them.' (Okay, maybe I saw this on a t-shirt, but somehow I have managed to weave it into my synapses as a memory.)

It does sound a bit cynical to call this the best phase of a boy–girl relationship. That would go to show that when it comes to relationships everyone has a terrible time. And that would be untrue. There are many people who are happy being in love. You know, the couples you look at and want to hurl in their general direction when you are alone and miserable. The ones who believe PDA is their civic right, the ones who indulge in baby talk (WHAT IS THAT!?), the ones who have cutesie nicknames (Poo Poo Bear/Jaanu) for each other, the ones who effortlessly make your brain want to commit suicide, those ones. But my point is that even though there is awareness, there is no understanding of it. That comes later. As do the pre-conceived notions, the expectations, the insecurities, the demands and so forth.

This is a time of scooters, learning how to read,

craving to own a watch, swinging the highest on a swing, going fastest on the merry go round, getting bitten by bees because you forgot there was a mini beehive on the doorbell, first school plays, running downhill really fast, falling, scraping your knees, getting a D, getting an A, getting chewing gum stuck in your hair, learning to tie your shoelaces and not having them open a minute later, being able to run to your mother for anything (this stays a constant, though).

These are our worries.

These are our triumphs.

And this is our world.

These are the days of not staying up late. For any reason.

This time is weightless. You are light on your feet and light in your heart.

Of course, you are going to romanticize every factor that made it a tangible whole. Everything seems perfect in retrospect. Hence, the phase of boy–girl relationship fits under that perfect parasol. What happens next depends on several factors.

We reach a crossroad. This is the part where we are growing up. Or deciding not to grow up. We pick a road and glide through it, or we pick a road and dig our heels in, refusing to move any further and wait for life to happen. And when life happens, and it scares us, we run like our head is on fire.

My teenage years were brilliant...

...ly disastrous.

But I didn't know that when it was happening to me. I thought that I was in the best phase of my life; things couldn't possibly get any better and I expected dancers to pirouette around me and hand me Virgin Coladas. I have no idea what road I chose when I came to that crossroad, but I do know that I glided through it. If I had another digit in my EQ, I would have done something about it. But life was too much fun. In my head. In spite of this, since awkwardness has a primordial pact with hormones to make every growing kid's life a nightmare at some point or the other, I spent one teenage year being awkward with myself, and the rest of the years being awkward with everyone else. It was all kinds of spectacular because I thought that it was a super power. It wasn't. And I only got that memo when I turned 23. And I gasped. For about six months. Then I wanted to build a time machine, go back to 1994, and Taser myself senseless for a decade.

What I did do in that interregnum nine-year period—allowing my personality to settle and dust itself off—is for another chapter.

3

Awkward

PERSONI.

The name of the lipstick, which made ~~witches~~ waves in 1995.

I spent the previous year hiding (I'll come to the lipstick in a bit). My teenage years can be roughly broken up into three phases. If I could line them up, I'd shoot them in the face without blindfolds.

Phase I began right after I left my cocoon in Assam where life was perfect. I'm not going to write about the perfect phase because everything perfect comes laced with a blanket of dullness. Let me tell you about what came after.

Teenage angst.

But it is never as simple as these two words strung together. These are the years of transitioning from girl to woman and boy to man. And the changes are far from just physical. Teenage angst is a complex berserker that is fuelled by chemical changes brought out in the body. These are some of the things that come into play outwardly:

- Untidiness
- Self consciousness
- Moodiness
- Love for all things loud (clothes + music + accessories)
- Rudeness

Now all these factors can happen all at once or appear as different permutations and combinations of a select few. I chose to go with love for all things loud and self consciousness. This was the base of my Phase I. Here are some details.

Phase I

I had been plucked out of a jungle in Assam and sent to hell for a whole year. Except, this hell was only mine. Even though I enrolled in school much later than I should have and technically only spent eight months at the Army Public School, Dhaula Kuan (Delhi), it felt like I was stuck in a time loop, where everyday was a repetition of the previous day, and the week became a swirl of days that were septuplets. I know this sounds terrifying (and fantastic at the same time!), but that's what it felt like. This was mostly because I had spent the past three years in something that seemed like it could have been home, but I had to leave it behind and start afresh, again, in a congested hot city, at an age where I was toying with the idea of being very self-conscious. Which, no matter how you look at, is a recipe for disaster.

I remember walking into school and hoping no one would notice me for the entire year. My plan was that if I kept very quiet, minded my own business and skulked around school like I was my own shadow, maybe I could be invisible. But that year I was the only new student in my class. And also, this was the phase when I was just getting to know My Awkward. Fourteen, buck-toothed, hirsute, friendless with the social skills of a prisoner in solitary confinement. My Awkward and I were just beginning to exchange pleasantries and hang out. I had no idea that we were going to become best friends over the next few years.

Fourteen going on 15, I had discovered boys and I loved all the cute ones (as one does) but since I didn't know what to do with this phenomenal discovery, I chose the technique of silently stalking from a distance. Not everyone gets lucky with love so easily yet I had the fortune of sitting behind a boy called Karan Nayyar. It was like winning a lottery for eight months, looking at it everyday, but never getting to spend it.

Karan had luscious black hair that he shaped into a bouffant at the front of his head. He was neither too short, nor too tall. He spoke in a jerky, staccato manner, which was very attractive. (To be honest, he could have spoken while drooling spinach soup and I would have found that attractive as well.) He carried a deodorant in his backpack and I knew this because I spent eight months staring at this backpack. He was perfect.

Month four and my first attempt at conversation with him.

'Hey. Do you know what time it is?'

'Ummm. You're wearing a watch, Juhi.'

My response was a gurgle. Which was me trying to swallow my own tongue to kill myself. I solemnly swore to myself to never initiate a conversation with a boy ever again.

Things looked up eventually. Beady eyed, I stayed silent for a few more months and during one free class, as I was making a paper plane, Karan walked into class and said, 'Ooh nice. Let's have a plane war.' And I heard that as 'I love you, Juhi'. So a few of us made a bunch of paper planes and threw them around in class. End of love story.

Karan and I never spoke again.

At the time I was certain I would never find love. But I'm also pretty sure every 14-year-old thinks that. Tragedies at that age are magnified. And to top it, this was a made-up tragedy, its building blocks being chunks of my own self-pity. Without having my heart broken I had a broken heart. I don't know what I was expecting. Maybe a conversation? A marriage proposal?

I wouldn't want to dive into the devious mind of a teenager swathed in excessive expectation. But love at this age is fleeting, especially when it is at a distance. All it took was a change of schools and the threatening dangers of high school to make my brain stop weeping. I would never forget Karan Nayyar. He was probably the only boy I'd had a conversation with who didn't look like an Ewok. Which is saying a lot. And for that, I am grateful.

Phase II

In the previous chapter I spoke about reaching a crossroad and choosing a path. I clearly didn't know there was a crossroad, so I just drifted along.

I finally got into a school that I had been aching to go to, and this was also the year that I had to take my board exams. This was a strange time in my life. I was trying to get out of the silent awkward zone and get into a slightly less silent awkward zone. Around this time I was subjected to all sorts of people in all sorts of shapes, sizes and personalities. This was because I had decided to open my eyes and try to like the environment I was in. I wasn't averse to this school or it's people (pre-conceived notions have a brilliant play on moods. It was very confusing to try and figure out which shape I fit in to. By now I had also decided that I was going to be tough and prove to the world that tomboys were people too. Mostly because I had assumed I was a tomboy because I didn't look like a girl.

Any girl.

From any species.

After shying away from people in general the year before, this new school of my choice had given me strength and I went and strapped on braces on my teeth. Once I knew I wasn't going to look like a hamster for much longer, I seized some self-confidence, but mostly in my room, alone and in front of the mirror. A step up is a step up.

I didn't have to worry about boy–girl relationships at this stage, because I continued to be the object of no one's desire. It's another thing that I was in love every week with a Nick Carter-look-alike, and it worked just fine that they didn't know my name. First or last. A whole year was spent summing up confidence and attempting to be nonchalant and it was great in theory, but I just couldn't get myself to practice any of it.

When I was asked my name, in theory, I was saying it with a slight sway of my head, in a low husky voice.

'Hey Juhi, want to play basketball?'

'Mmmmm. Yeah...sure...' I would say in a voice drenched in molten gold and honey.

But I wasn't asked that. IF I were, I knew my slow, drawly answer.

Though I was asked if I was in Mr Enas' sculpture class once.

'...'

'What?'

'Yes.'

That's right. I showed them.

I didn't. But I could have. If I just had more time.

If only I knew that I did have more, it would have made life so much easier. I would have not tried to rush into being a future me. I would have been less hard on myself and not practiced saying things to people repeatedly, in my head, in the right manner. I would have slowly eased into it. But then again, youth has an unrequired urgency for everything. In retrospect, I braced myself, and maybe I taught myself to keep digging and trying to find who I really was. And getting to know the silent introverted side of me, which would eventually give me a deep sense of empathy for years to come (I don't even step on ants if I can help it).

PHASE III

After a year of prepping myself for some kind of fantastic future, I cleared the class 10 boards, got three months off school, cut my hair, experimented shaving on one arm, hiked my skirt up, and spoke a lot. I was ready to be 17!

Enter Personi lipstick (told'ya I'd get to it). The rage of all feminine youth in the northern cities of India circa 1997. I felt empowered. I felt like a woman. I wore lipstick. I was now trendy, even though several striped tights/leggings had made their way into my wardrobe. I sometimes crimped my short hair to resemble a fibre optic vase. It's not like I was trying hard (I was). This was my idea of trying to fit in, with doing the exact opposite of what the world was.

Suck at math?

Take up math.

Suck at art?

Take up art.

Suck at basketball?

Take up basketball.

I stuck out like a sore thumb and my brain was getting fatigued with all these new fangled things. But I wasn't going to give up. I was on a quest. I didn't know what the quest was, but I'm going to say self-discovery.

Mostly everyone had a boyfriend by the time they were 17 or 18. Or at least had someone who liked them. I didn't have either. Sometimes that sucked. Mostly because all the boys I secretly liked (loved) didn't know I existed. And even if they did, I was that girl with the funny hair and braces. Like when I didn't get asked to dance at the continuation party of the class 12 farewell, I thought my life was over. It was incredibly depressing. I had worn red bell-bottom jeans, a black faux leather jacket zipped up to my neck and black boots. Surely this was a man-magnet. Were they all blind? Did they wish they were? If not, then why was I the only one sitting in the corner of a room with a glass of Fanta?

Right after this deathly depressing episode, exams hit me square in the face and last-minute panic made me study. I cleared my exams and suddenly I was out of school. Bam! It was done. At 18, I walked into adulthood with zero expectation. That's like walking into a warzone with a bodysuit made of Kevlar. It was pretty amazing. I stopped trying to be someone and let go of that obsession. I got rid of my gimmicky wardrobe (four different coloured stripes on tights with giant red sweaters. That's right). I threw away that heinous dark brown Personi lipstick, which gave me a cadaverish look, and I learnt how to shave my arms (both of them). And because I was used to severe amounts of heartbreak (on account of not being noticed), I stopped caring.

It was like walking on air. Everything felt new. I was going to go to college to a new city, I made some new friends outside of school and I got a summer job at a store, which meant I was going to be rich. I had nothing to complain about. I was still awkward, but in a very subtle manner. If someone paid me a compliment and I was drinking something, that thing would squirt out of my nose because I would choke. But I was a far cry from the girl who walked into high school hoping not be noticed.

As for love, I had given up on it. I stopped thinking about it. Sure there were cute boys, but I was now okay with the idea that none of them were riding towards me on a steed to whisk me away. This made life easy. Zero hope. Zero expectation. And so much to do and see if you weren't getting your heartbroken (even if it was imaginary heartbreak).

In a span of four years I had learnt the art of accepting failure and rejection as a part of life and not something that just happened to me. As morose as this may sound it is actually a weapon. I liked math, didn't mean I could ace it. And I had to live with that. Same with basketball. Same with boys. It was okay for me to have a crush on someone and not have them reciprocate (even though they didn't know I had a crush on them). I'm not saying I was okay with failure/rejection. I'm saying that I realized that this was how things worked. We don't always get what we want and I was okay with the idea, at least for the time being.

There would come a phase when I would expect a lot because I gradually grew used to having a lot, and then be disappointed and have my entire world spin out of control. But that is called a quarter-life crises and it is much worse than the Black Death.

At the threshold of adulthood I was just excited. New things and places have that effect on me. Glee is a word I'd like to use but it would make me sound like a toddler, so I'll let you make up a more mature word.

But after years of tiring trial and error, I had given up on the experiment and decided to just jump right into what life had to offer me without trying to fit any cookie cutter mold.

To sum it up, I would say that awkwardness is not something I hope everyone goes through. It's grueling. But if you do/have, take from it. Take whatever silver lining it threw at you and wrap yourself in it. If nothing else, at least you'll look like a human disco ball. And who doesn't like a human disco ball?

4

Bad Boys

EVEN AS I AM WRITING THE TITLE OF THIS CHAPTER I can't wipe the smile off of my face. Bad boys—two little words that can look good just put on paper and seem... dangerous. I have never understood my (and I speak for most women) fascination with bad boys. All through school, college, my early twenties, late twenties...heck forever, the bad boys have always taken centrestage. Perhaps, that's because they can.

From the moment Mickey Anand walked into school with his high cheekbones, long hair, pierced ears and denim cut offs, life changed. For me and about 600 other girls in senior school. Ours was a school that believed in uniforms, short hair, no earrings, and definitely no chewing on gum while talking to the teachers. And what did Mickey Anand do? All of the above *and* he looked nonchalant while doing it. For two whole years that he was in school, he did whatever pleased him and looked absolutely carefree through it all. We don't know how he got away with the long hair, but I guess the teachers must have just blushed when he came up with an excuse made up of words like 'curse', 'firstborn', 'long hair', 'essential', diseased sharks', or something equally daft. He didn't look very intelligent, but I don't think any of us cared about his IQ level. Just watching him play basketball was poetic enough.

He played basketball during math class.

He played basketball during English class.

He played basketball during accounts class.

Well, he played basketball all day and no one said a word to him. Had it been me playing basketball during PE class, I'd get hauled up. But that was probably because I looked shady. He wasn't the quintessential bad boy because I don't think he went about getting into fights, but he was almost there with his rule flouting. And that worked for all 600 of us who were constantly swooning over him. This just goes to show that when you're a certain age, intelligence in the opposite sex has very little to do with attraction. I'm certain I loved him for a few months. As did all my friends. After a while of moseying along, he fell in love with the most beautiful girl in school and they started dating. I immediately swapped love for hate and continued with my life thinking it was his loss. Not mine.

This is just an innocent example of a bad boy in high school. Things change and get serious as you grow up. Bad boys aren't just the guys who turn up late for class with a lopsided grin and have the ability to unknowingly make girls fall in love with them. They come in different guises and sometimes end up wrecking your life because you are too busy falling for the exterior charm and indifferent attitude. The two qualities which you will learn to hate in the coming years. They can be uncaring, selfish, and some of them even realize that if they treat you bad long enough, not only do you get used to it but you also end up with very low self esteem fueling their already inflated ego a little bit more. And this becomes the beginning of a downward spiral.

These 'bad boys' will remove whoever is on centrestage and take the spotlight for themselves. Rules mean very little to them, so they either break them or don't care much about them. These are one of the many traits that constitute an alpha male personality type. If we look at a broader definition, an alpha male is typically an aggressive, highly ranked man in a group. And most 'bad boys' are primarily alpha males without allowing a smidgen of the good attributes to peep through. The façade is replete with dollops of charm and a fair amount of bad boy-ness (read unfaithfulness) that then leads to a conflict with their partner(s). It's a typical moth to a flame ideology, where what you are attracted to destroys you.

All said and done, there arises the vital question—

why would a woman, any woman, intelligent, independent, attractive woman willingly get into a relationship with a bad boy? A relationship that will eventually sour and become toxic. It starts out with a passion that most are unfamiliar with. You're not really attracted to this person because of their wisdom or how comfortable they make you feel. You're in it because of the sweaty palms, the slight nervousness, lust and generally not knowing what's going to happen next. There is an aura of unpredictability around him. It's thrilling to be around this person because the excitement is always palpable initially. This is all pretty fantastic, till of course, it isn't. It goes from a heady, wide-eyed fervour to something tedious that you can't deal with. The casualness of it all, the general disregard of things and people, the frequent aggression loses its charm and everything eventually nose dives. For you. The 'every day bad boy' is not something you were expecting. Somehow, in the back of your mind you thought it would be different once you were together, that things would change or better still, he would change. Instead, things get out of hand, you realize that the nonchalance is just selfishness in disguise, that you don't feature very high in the list of priorities, lies are frequent till you wonder if anything coming out of his mouth isn't just fantasy.

And before you know it, you're way down the rabbit hole. And to top it, you're a mess. Your judgment is weak, because if it wasn't, then you wouldn't be in this situation. Along with your judgment your self esteem has decided to slay itself, leaving you in a situation you only thought other people got into. It's not a pretty sight. And to pick up the pieces and make yourself whole again is like putting together a 3000-piece jigsaw puzzle in the dark. Not easy.

Quite frankly I won't be able to give you a list of answers or for that matter, any answer about why rational women fall hook, line, and sinker for these men who are not really what they want. The reasons could be many, ranging from 'I couldn't get over his calf muscles' to 'I think I fell for him when he punched me in the sternum'. Seriously though, if you dive deeper, psychologically the reasons might touch upon lack of self confidence, an absentee father, hormones, the need to save them (from themselves) or a combination of any of the above. Another study discusses our need for unpredictability which then leads to unanticipated rewards thus giving way to more dopamine release, which as we all know is a feel-good hormone. Whatever the reason, the Bad Boy Syndrome is something that most girls experience at least once in their life. How you deal with it is what is interesting.

You could get swayed by it all and fall in love. Which is fine, but I think it's love only if you are loved back without any ulterior motives. And these ulterior motives could be as simple as needing you around as a security blanket. I was once told that 'You have to be euphoric when you're in love. This is the part where you don't have any worries. This other person is supposed to make you fall in love with life.' And though this may not be possible every single day, there needs to be an undercurrent of this emotion at all times. A whisper, a sense, a feeling of general well being even when the world around you is crumbling. Why else would you choose to be with someone? If you have to feel miserable, wouldn't you just rather re-visit your childhood with your sibling (especially the part where they locked you in the bathroom for hours or stabbed you in your thigh with a compass)? Your partner needs to get the best out of you. This is a fact. Whether or not it can be exercized doesn't stop it from being a fact. Or rather it should be an axiom. Something that you consider when in a relationship. The moment you start coming up with excuses to explain someone's behaviour, you know that the axiom is looking at you with a frown and saying 'Really??'

The same goes for women. All of this can be applied

to either sex. It's like a reversible sweater with a really bizarre design.

Also, just because someone doesn't love you back, doesn't give them an honorary position in the Bad Boy Club. Say for example, after mustering up enough courage, you tell a boy you're secretly in love with 'I think I'm in love with you' and he turns around and says 'Aww. That's cute. I'm not', it doesn't make him anything but a brutally honest person. It doesn't add any extra swagger to his walk, or more hair to his already balding pate. All it does is make you look a little stupid because you assumed the person *you* 'loved' would love you back. You don't always get what you want and that should be something that you should be willing to accept and learn to live with. Though I must give ~~myself~~ the person who has been able to do this 10 points for summing up the courage to go pour ~~my~~ her heart out. Life isn't all vanilla ice cream with chocolate chips sprinkled on top. And even if it is, some people have sensitive teeth because they brush too often. This last sentence is supposed to make some kind of sense but since it does not, do what you will with it.

Then there are some bad boys who are actually sheep in wolf's clothing. And I don't think it can better than this. This type generally has a tough exterior, is unaffected by estrogen, with a couldn't-give-a-damn look, obscenely good looking by default, and has the soul of a newborn kitten tucked away somewhere. This, honestly, is pure gold. You get treated right, by guys who look like the guys who would never treat you right. It's usually a win-win situation as long as you don't blow their cover.

Not everyone gets lucky enough to date this bad (good) boy because most times you can't really tell the difference. The process of trial and error with this situation is not really worth the effort. So if you luck out, you luck out. It's a game of Russian roulette where the odds aren't really in your favour. If this sounds too morbid I could balance it out by writing an entire chapter about leprechauns.

If we're smart enough, at some point in our life, this irrational obsession of bad boys eventually ends and we settle for something less damaging. If it doesn't end, then no amount of friends or family can try to talk us out if it, hours spent staring at the mirror and knowing we're making a mistake, or calling it a phase is going to help. You're going to have to ride that storm exactly how you want it, and if you want it rough, rough is what you will get.

Maybe when wisdom comes and kicks you in the teeth, and your brain stops aching to be 17, the bad boys take a back seat. They stop being an obsession, your heart stops skipping beats when they walk by, and they end up being what they're really good at—easy on the eyes. And when you're at a distance, you can kick back and relax and know that you're invincible. (Only to the bad boys. I'm pretty certain other terrible things can happen to you.) That you are not going to get sucked into the vortex, that you have treaded the dreaded path and come out wiser. That you can appreciate a good (bad) thing, without wanting in.

I'm not saying you will be immune to attraction. That is not a possibility. But when you know someone's game, it becomes exactly that. A game. And every game has a predictive quality about it. A discerning mind will not run to it at breakneck speed.

I don't think I wanted to be cautious all through my twenties. That was just boring. There's a time in your life when you like train wrecks so much that you want to be them. And you're really successful at it. If only you put in this much energy into...anything else, you would have aced that. You could have been a successful flautist, or learnt French, or understood permaculture. Instead you chased a boy who didn't chase you back, and so you sulked and moped and felt miserable. All this looks so simple in retrospect, and if you had to make a decision now, it would be a no brainer. But back then it was not retrospect. It was as real as your foot stuck in a bear trap. And maybe as painful.

Some boys who make you jelly-kneed from a distance, should remain at a distance.

Again, this is knowledge that comes from experience. Because when you're in it, let's face it, it feels pretty damn right. So I guess the bottom line is riding that wave, and if you crash a few times you need to take up another sport. Surfing looks really good, but it's tough work and not for the weak.

5

First Love/Heartbreak

THE BEST/WORST THING TO HAPPEN TO GIRLS IN ALL time, in all parts of the world is the First Love/ Heartbreak phenomenon.

There's usually a sequence of events but the beginnings are always about unmatched euphoria and the ends unimaginable pain. If only we knew that this is going to be a 'lather, rinse, repeat' situation we would probably handle it a little better with all the drama dialed down a bit. But nobody gives us the memo. If our mothers or friends or aunts or anybody else even attempts to hand us any advice in the matter, we usually want to draw blood. That's the beauty of First Love/Heartbreak. It's overkill at a nuclear level.

It's inevitable.

It's full of action and drama.

It's a movie waiting to happen with its very own hero and heroine.

If there were a soundtrack to this it would be done by Pharell Williams.

A lot of people walk in slo-mo during this phenomenon

(Or so they'd like to perceive)

Everyone is happy for the most part and then people start to cry. Even the boys.

It's amazing and it's terrible. It could also be called *Pacific Rim* (insert any movie that you've been ashamed to love).

What can I say; it's brilliant to fall in love for the first time. It can't compare to anything that may have happened in your life before. It's a heady cocktail of dopamine, serotonin, and oxytocin rushing through your veins, so why wouldn't you feel on top of the world?! The person you're in love with is the *best* thing that has ever happened to you and he loves you back! That's like dessert and some more dessert, right after a buffet of dessert.

It feels like this is going to last forever because this person makes you the happiest in the world, and your friends/family/school/college/work/everything else fades to black. You have tunnel vision and all you can see is your lover.

This is great. If only one could slam the brakes and hang on to this feeling forever, everything would be just peachy. (Don't get me wrong. I know a few people who've been in love from the moment they laid eyes on each other. And they need a standing ovation and all our jealousy directed at them.) But nine times out of ten, this doesn't happen.

During the course of the good part of your first love affair/shenanigan, your boyfriend will be a shaken and stirred version of Ryan Gosling in his Hey Girl mode and Prince Harry (in any mode). When you walk into your first relationship you feel like a new person. A version of you that you knew existed, but could never tap into because you didn't know how to. With this boy/man in your life you're suddenly the best combination of your inner Greta Garbo and Gwen Stefani. That tomboy? She's long gone. Instead there's you. Version 2 point Ooh!

I can only throwback to my first love. I remember that my first relationship really helped me be less uncomfortable and surer of myself, and things around me in general. Love gives you that power. Especially when it is positive. And aren't all first loves positive? First date, first movie, first dance, first kiss, first sitting in a cab together, first rain, first summer, first dhokla, first first first. Why wouldn't it be fantastic?

Boys can be just the right kind of charming when they need to be. They bring out the best in you when they want to. And the same goes for us. We do the same for them. So I'm not going to try and make this into some kind of a boy-bashing situation. I have always maintained that most relationships are based on the action–reaction theory.

You get into your first relationship not treading

carefully. But the first few months set precedence for expectation. And because the colour from the nouveau rose-tinted glasses eventually wears off, all we see is our expectation, which we never thought we had, lying shattered on the floor.

There could be so many reasons for your disappointment.

- You never thought you were capable of jealousy.
- You never thought you could make someone jealous.
- You never thought you'd have to hear someone whine.
- You never realized how much YOU whined.
- You want time alone.
- You can't understand why he would want time alone. You're awesomesauce.
- You sometimes don't get him or his ideas.
- You're confused when he doesn't get you.
- Even though you're a champ at ignoring calls, suddenly you can't understand him not calling you back immediately.
- You let the phone ring incessantly to teach him a lesson.
- You can't understand why he needs to have other girl friends.
- He starts questioning you about all your guy friends.

- He doesn't give you any attention.
- He gives you too much attention.

And that's the way the cookie crumbles. The cracks emerge, and at that nubile young age of first relationships and inexperience, they usually widen pretty fast.

These simple problems, if swaddled with enough rage, can give rise to some, how shall I put it, tempestuous moments. About a decade and a half ago I may or may not have smashed a windshield of a car, while possibly screaming so loud that it's a wonder someone didn't wrap me up in a straitjacket. On another occasion I may or may not have thrown a cellphone from a moving car and then tried to jump out myself. All young people should carry a horse tranquilizer in a syringe, in their back pockets at all times. For themselves.

Our first loves are a gateway drug. It is our initiation into a world of man–woman complexities. We are emotional beings who, most times, work on different frequencies. The differences of these frequencies only come to light when all the rainbows and unicorns have trotted off into a sunset and we're left with the real deal. Which isn't necessarily bad. It's just that we're not expecting reality. We want our Mr Darcy everyday.

There are many ways that girls show their displeasure.

- **There is the Silent Treatment,** which I know for a fact that every girl has used on being miffed. Even though I have as well, I've never understood how it really helps. I think it's a knee-jerk reaction for women, but it doesn't really do...anything, aside from making matters a few fold worse. I once managed to stay silent/sulk for seventy-two hours. By the end of it, it seemed like a race that I was winning. I just didn't know what the prize was. I found out later that it was angst, confusion, zero clarity, and shrieking decibels. That's how the silent treatment eventually ends up solving problems. Like a 3-year-old. So, unless you're a Jedi-trained in the art of mind reading, don't bother with this nerve-bursting trick.

- **Then there is the screaming and shouting.** And we know how that turns out. Screaming and shouting solves every problem. This is a lie. It doesn't. But you knew that. You've known that all along, but instead, you squash your IQ and rage without your lungs tiring.

- **Taunt.** This is a word that should be removed from our vocabulary. Just looking at it makes me cringe. It's just a bad word with a bad meaning. And it's used all the time. Not the word, the action. The act of provoking someone or hurting them just because you're not happy with a particular situation. This is where evolution sits up, takes notice, packs its bags and takes off, and Darwin turns in his grave. If you think about it rationally, you will realize the futility of taunting someone, especially if it's someone you love. But then again, raging and being eaten alive with anger leaves little time for rationality.

If your first relationship lasts a while, then you either learn from these things, or you remain stubborn and continue, hoping that someone will catch on to what you're feeling (more often than not that someone is you).

After it has run its course, for reasons known only to you, the relationship ends. Sometimes it's amicable. Most times it is not. There is either a fight or a discussion. There is a lie that is found out, or an attraction that comes to light. The reasons are many and not my business. But once the relationship ends, it takes a while to sink in. It's a sadness that is all enveloping. A black cloud of despair, which you wrap around yourself like a favourite cloak. Nothing makes sense any more. The person you gave your heart to, wrapped up with all your innocence and twinkling eyes, is not with you anymore and has left you with a taste of betrayal that you will not forget soon (ever).

Maybe it was your fault.

Maybe it was not your fault.

Maybe there was no fault, but it was time.

All that matters is that it's over and it's never coming back. And as much as women like to tell themselves that we feel more than the other sex, in their defense I'd like to differ. Just because they don't voice it as much (to the other sex: showing your pain is a clear sign that you're full of estrogen and one step short of getting boob implants) doesn't mean that this is the end of something special for them as well.

How am I an authority on men? If I rip my ribcage open right now, I'll still find the tomboy that I left behind a decade ago. By virtue of that, I have several men in my life that I count as my closest friends and I have seen them become weak and crumble, in their own subtle manner, at the end of a relationship (first, second, or otherwise). They may not necessarily weep, but weeping isn't the only indication of sadness.

Heartbreak is tough. Your first heartbreak is probably the toughest. You feel like you'll never recover from that gaping hole in your soul. And maybe you will carry a little bit of it all your life. Someone once said, 'Only unrequited love is romantic.' If that be the case, then that tiny flame of romance should stay burning deep inside us for as long as it can. Why deny yourself that? It doesn't necessarily have to scar you. It might take some time, but it can be put in the fond memory cabinet inside your head. Sure, when it is actually happening to you the searing pain is incomparable.

Then begins the quest to get over it. But before that comes hatred (not in some cases, of course. Let's hope that spewing venom isn't step 2 of heartbreak for everyone). You have to hate the boy who broke your heart. It's basic mathematics. And even if you don't want to go down that road, your friends are going to make sure that you do.

How could he?

You deserve better.

You dodged a bullet.

He was such a douche in any case.

None of us actually liked him.

You were too good for him.

He's going to realize his mistake and come crawling back.

Don't ever talk/text/call/email/snapchat him ever again.

The anger phase is directly proportionate to the level of jilt in the jilted lover. The more, the angrier. Once that tide washes over you and you deal with it by:

a) Hating all men
b) The opposite of hating all men
c) Deciding never to fall in love
d) Deciding to fall in love all the time
e) Being rational and going about your life acting like several thousand years of evolution has made some impact on you

Option e would be the way to go but how many of us actually do that? Basic instincts are much stronger than 'calm the hell down, there is a way out of this without harassing your neurons too much'.

My route was to cry for an entire day and a night. Then I decided to play Ostrich (did you know that ostriches don't actually dig their heads under the sand to hide?). I was going to be done with this entire matter of heartbreak as soon as I was done crying, which took about twenty-four hours. After which I was fine. I went to work (which I had just started ten days before), I worked nine hours, I went and met my friends. They didn't say anything to me but I knew they were staring when I wasn't looking. I laughed a little, went home, felt normal, had my parents walk on eggshells around me, expecting me to start bawling, but I didn't bawl and went to bed instead.

Three months later, I reacted to my repressed break-up like a regular irrational human being. I was normal. Anger, hate, self pity, swearing never to be in love again, boys are bastards, I'm above this, hate hate hate, oooh look alcohol, I like discotheques, I want to be alone, I don't want to work, I only want to work, I love my friends, my friends are scheming bastards they only want me unhappy, I'm going to cut my hair, I think grunge is back.

Yep. I did it all. I behaved like the 20-year-old I was and I fit into the cookie cutter mould of a first heartbreak reaction. If I had to go back and do it over again, would I do it any different? I don't think so. I think it's essential to feel a surge of various emotions because you have had no learning/training of this process. And no one can tell you how to feel or how to be. It's something you teach yourself, this being the first step of many.

I recently read *The Fault in Our Stars* by John Green. I didn't think I'd like it that much. It's a beautiful tragedy about love, and the sentence that spoke most to my X chromosome was 'Oh, I wouldn't mind, Hazel Grace. It would be a privilege to have my heart broken by you.'

It would be nice to fast forward to a few years later and feel that way about your first love (heartbreak notwithstanding).

6

Oh Look! Unicorn!

DIS.TRAC.TION

/dis'trakSHən/

Noun

A thing that prevents someone from giving full attention to something else.

If you were me, and the world was always a glass that was half full instead of half empty, then you would look at distraction as a virtue. I have graduated in two different fields of study, worked in five different industries (I'm onto my sixth), and I tend to have a new hobby every couple of years that I refuse to excel at. My career graph (and hobby fascination) would be a Jackson Pollock painting if it were ever put down on canvas.

A lot of straight-laced people would probably disapprove of my multiple choices when it comes to work, play, and social circles. And to them I say, 'Get back to your desk and push that paper.' I don't want to trivialize or glorify distraction. I want to treat it as something that certain people have an affinity for. In fact, another way of looking at it would be to consider yourself a polymath or at least a person with the potential to be a polymath. (Sometimes there is too much forced focus in one concentrated area of study/work. This squashes the chances of having a wider variety of interests. The thirst for knowledge/expertise is more linear than broad, thereby leading to the death of the polymath.) And if you do happen to have that affinity, embrace it. Because when it is time to stop getting distracted, you will.

I think it was a matter of classical conditioning that lead to my love for distraction. I had to change schools every year because of my father changing squadrons or aircrafts in the Air Force. What could have been a cause for 'separation anxiety' and 'displacement' in regular kids was my standard school year. Except that I got to go to a new place, explore it, stare at its people, make friends, not make friends, and generally have a whole new adventure every twelve months. I think this percolated a little deeper as I grew up. Every new place would lead me to new things. I spent two years chasing art and aiming to be an artist. Then it was sculpture. Then it was learning the piano. And a sprinkling of other 'YOU DON'T UNDERSTAND! THIS IS WHAT I'M GOING TO BE WHEN I GROW UP' things.

At some point, I realized that I might be running out

of time, and since I wanted to be so many things in one go, I figured I might as well try to do them all at once. If not, at least spend every waking hour trying to learn everything about them. So, I did hotel management, along with applied nutrition, I studied psychology and philosophy and I took weekend classes to know more about event management. Basically, I took the most fun years of transitioning from a teenager to an adult, collected them like dry twigs, heaped them together, and set them on fire.

At no point did I look at this as distraction or consider myself attention deficit. I took everything I did very seriously and I did a fairly good job of it. It is not essential to give names or tags to things or habits, especially if those names lean to an assumed negative connotation. And the same can be applied to relationships, to men.

Remember that incredibly dull accounts class where the profit and loss statement seemed like a bottomless pit that could swallow your soul in one breath? Remember casually looking out of the window out of deathly boredom for just a second? Remember suddenly catching a glimpse of that incredibly cute boy taking a stroll around the school campus? Remember that sudden interest in life again? Remember feeling rejuvenated and ready to tackle the world and your accounts class with a newfound love for balance sheets?

That is distraction too.

Of course, it doesn't always retain such innocence. Sometimes things get messy. You could be in a relationship and fall for someone else. Would that be considered distraction? Sure. Would it be okay to leave who you're with and chase after the shiny new object? It's your life; you can do as you please, though you would need to question your basis for flitting away. At that moment logic wouldn't be at the forefront of your thoughts, but in case it is, it would be nice to have a dialogue and act like an adult. Nine times out of ten this won't happen till much later. But then emotions like guilt and remorse also get involved and things get morose.

Here is a set of questions, which you should ask yourself when you're about to do said crime. (Observe how it's moved from distraction to crime in a matter of four sentences.)

1. Are you distracted because you have spent far too much time in your current relationship and things have become mundane?
2. Are you distracted because you've fallen out of love?
3. Are you distracted because your boyfriend wears crocs and you're this close to setting his head on fire?

4. Are you distracted because you didn't consider all factors before getting into this relationship and were just happy that someone liked you?
5. Is the object of your new affection Ryan Gosling from *Place Behind the Pines*?
6. Is the object of your new affection an Abercrombie & Fitch model with an IQ level that is a single digit number?
7. Do you need constant excitement and is your current situation not giving you that?
8. Are you a commitment-phobe?
9. What's the sound of one hand clapping?
10. Are you and your boyfriend a complete mismatch and has it taken you some time to figure it out?
11. Are you stupid?

Once you tackle these questions and come to a decision that there's a possibility that you might have fallen out of love and do not want to be in your current relationship, go ahead and take all measures to exit from it. There is nothing wrong in bowing out of a situation that doesn't make you happy. Which is possibly the reason why you were getting attracted to the other person in the first place. But, if after giving it a lot of thought you realize that you are actually in love and can't do without your partner, then work on the relationship.

A lot of times people get set in their ways and things get routine, and that has the ability to suck the joy out of anything. 'If you think adventure is dangerous, try routine; it is lethal.' I wish I had come up with this quote, but then I'd have to change my name to Paulo Coelho. But that line sums it up. If it is because of routine that your life seems bleak, tackle that, forget the distraction, and do everything in your power to make yourself happy.

Whatever you choose to do won't be easy. Why should it be? Life has a way of making you work really hard for the things you want. Whether it's breaking up with someone, or trying to make it work with them. One makes you the primordial bitch and the other makes you exhausted. But in the end, you will have a cleaner slate, or a slate that has a nice drawing of a dinosaur or dragon (insert drawing of choice).

I have used various forms of distraction. I've had my work, I've had travel, I've had my studies, I've eyed some boys and I've managed to play Ostrich by burying my head in the sand (which is not something ostrichs do, but whatever) and refusing to look up and face reality. I've always tried to use the method of 'If there's a problem, ignore it or work around it, till it explodes in your face and everything is ruined.' Let me tell you, it hasn't been fun. Which is why I can afford to get really preachy in this chapter. Because I have tried all the 'Don'ts' from the list of Dos and Don'ts and I've realized that they don't work.

I once tried to solve a situation by running away to the mountains. Fifteen days of clean air, couple of amazing friends, treks, good food, making new weird friends, trying to get rid of them, planning great things for the future, erasing the past. I tried to do it all in a fortnight. And it worked. I had forgotten about my situation back on terra firma, and I was happy as a bee. This lasted about a month.

The thing I've come to understand is that you can run, but you can't hide (I need to stop watching the *I Know What You Did Last Summer* movies). The problems are in your head and not with a place or an area code.

The most that running away will give you is clarity (and momos). And if you get that clarity you still have a lot of dirty work to do to fix whatever it is that you were running away from. No amount of standing and staring at a woman shoving a pen up her nose to make it vanish is going to magically untangle your life. Even if it was in the middle of a bustling city centre in Leh. (She had some cartilage missing, it was a medical thing, but she could put a pen up her nose without damaging anything. It was cool and gross.)

That's the thing about distraction. It is necessary for

a little while. It helps put things in perspective and it gives you that slight respite that might be needed to look at the bigger picture, that slight intangible distance that is required to get a bird's eye view of the master plan. But distraction is never the solution. It is the means to the solution. Though sometimes, it is mistaken as the answer, which is when we falter and expect something out of it, which was never going to be the case.

Distraction has its place in life. It's essential to use it once in a while in situations that are tricky and confusing. It is a wonderful device that might actually open our mind to different ideas, thoughts, and solutions. Of course, there are times when we are unaware of our distraction and just go with the flow. At some point when the recognition seeps in, we should use it to our advantage.

At no point do I want to insinuate that life should be a series of calculated steps, but sometimes it is essential to solve a problem with the right algorithm.

And if all else fails, there's always this.

'Immersing oneself in the problems of a book is a good way to keep from thinking of love.'—Orhan Pamuk, *Snow*

7

Romeo

LET ME TELL YOU A LITTLE FAIRYTALE.

Tea met Romeo many years ago...in her head. Her mind had taken a long time to curate him. He was tall and, of course, good looking. He had equal measures of wit and charm, and he rarely relied on sarcasm, but when he did, it was razor sharp. He walked with a slight swagger, his hair was floppy but never unkempt. And most importantly he adored Tea in ways Tea had only dreamed of, because let's face it, he *was* really a dream.

Wouldn't it be fantastic if he were real? These were thoughts that Tea would have fleetingly. But since Romeo was just her imagination, she knew that he would never really turn into a reality.

Tea went through life as one does. She finished college, started work, got a new hobby, made some new friends, reconnected with the old ones, travelled a little, partied a lot, met some interesting men, some not so interesting men, broke a few hearts, had hers broken. It was textbook. And because it was textbook, there came a point where drudgery set in. Every now and then she would go back to thinking about Romeo. The fantasy that he might actually be real, that the placidity of her life would take a hike if he were real. The sun would shine brighter, the leaves would rustle and whisper, the spring in her step would be absurdly like a pogo stick on crack, her smile would be more genuine because she had a reason to smile all the time. Wouldn't this love be grand?

At the movies one day, Tea's friend brought along someone she worked with. His name was Romeo. Tea started to blush just at the mention of his name. There was no reason for her to blush because she didn't even know this man. He was tall, he was handsome in a rugged sort of way, and he spoke softly but surely and was very polite. Tea couldn't focus on the movie the entire time. She was very aware that Romeo was sitting two seats away from her. He seemed like the Romeo in her head. She had never really given a face to her Romeo, but at that moment she was pretty sure that if she had, he would look exactly like the Romeo sitting an arm's distance away.

What if...

Could it be...

Should she dare even think like that?

The movie whizzed past her on warp speed. At the end of it, she walked out expecting something. A sign, a hint, a threat. Something. Anything. Sure enough, just as she was leaving, Romeo turned to her and said that they should catch up for a movie again sometime soon.

Stars exploded, as did Tea's head. Sure, she said nonchalantly, trying not to grin like Eddie Murphy from *Bowfinger*. He asked for her number, she gave it. And before she got home she received a text from Romeo that said: this is me!

And so the texting story began. The remnants of the Romeo in her head got together like mercury and took whatever little she knew of this new real life Romeo and fused them together to make for a real life figment of imagination.

Things were great. Romeo liked her. She liked Romeo. They went for movies, they went to the park, they went for drives, and they took a small holiday, all in the span of three months. Cherubs were cherubing, birds were tweeting. These were times when Tea never had a bad hair day, and if she smiled anymore she'd swallow her own head. It was so perfect that it was one step shy of being a horror film. And then it happened.

Things started to slow down a bit. The initial euphoria started to die down. Everyday life started to seep into the manic bubble of love. Little things that Tea hadn't even thought of before started to peep out from everywhere. Like Romeo's habit of picking his teeth with a toothpick constantly. It used to fall under the 'Oh my god that is so sexy I'm going to die' category till a few weeks ago, and now it was in the 'Oh my God I want to die right now' category. Sometimes Romeo would get really excited while talking, and in that excitement end up spitting on the other person. Just a tiny spray of saliva. For the first month Tea thought that this was really cute. Month two she still thought it was cute. Month three, she thought that maybe he had a problem. And on month four it was all about looking for the nearest umbrella. Cute went away. Babies are cute. Puppies are cute. Some raccoons are cute. Spitting while talking isn't cute. It's the opposite of cute. And that's what Tea realized.

Suddenly, all these tiny, annoying habits started to gather together and come at Tea like a waterfall of mistakes, and this confused her. She had spent so much time working on the Romeo in her head, and then after meeting the real life Romeo, spent so much time equating him to the made up Romeo, that she forgot to separate one from the other. When she made up the Romeo in her head, she did not give him any flaws. Why would she? Who even does that? Imaginary people are meant to be perfect. That aside, Tea started to realize that even if Romeo was perfect, he was perfect too late.

Had she met him earlier, and not become so set in

her ways, could things have been different? Maybe she wouldn't have wanted to take a bat to his face every time he mispronounced 'Mercedes'. Maybe cringing wouldn't have been her default expression. Tea wondered whether this was her fault or if she could pin the blame on time. Had she grown out of the ideal image she had created in her mind? Could it be that simple and tragic? What of young romance? What of Romeo?

Romeo clearly didn't know what he had done wrong. He was just going ahead and being who he was. He had no idea that every single day he was letting Tea down. Every move he made, every time he spoke, there was something in his tone, the way his mouth moved, or the fact that he liked to drag his feet a little, was pushing Tea away a little. He could see her withdraw. Their once long conversations were now barely skeletal. She had slowly switched from talking incessantly to using a lot of hmms. But the last three months had been fantastic, so Romeo let it slide, thinking it a phase. But as time passed by, Tea remained the same. Sometimes he would feel her watching him. Even in a regular conversation. He felt like he was trapped in a petri dish. Tiny little Romeo germ being watched under an intense microscope. So he started to try harder. You know when you pull a slingshot and it misses and hits your hand? Yeah. That happened. Tea couldn't take it anymore. There were fights, but these fights were not direct. These fights were about things concerning their goldfish not being fed on time. Verbal fights with enough intensity to blow up a city. He figured something was up, and no amount of asking what was wrong would get him the answer.

Could Tea actually have the strength to tell him that she wasn't in love with him? Could she do that? Tell him that she's not in love with him and that it was actually a BIG mistake? That she rushed into it? That 'Hey, don't get me wrong, but the real you kinda sucks, so I'm going to head out. Take care of yourself. Click Click Boom'?

Yeah. I didn't think so. Therefore it got manifested into fights. About subjects that could only be classified under 'Silly'.

- Why didn't you feed the fish? Everything can't be my responsibility!
- This is OUR pet. Not just mine.
- You took my bicycle lock without asking me. I had to take the bus. I don't understand why you have to be so selfish!!!
- Why didn't you lock the door? You came home after me. You should have locked it. If we get murdered in our sleep it will be because you are careless.
- I did the plates last night; it's your turn now. Why do I have to tell you this?

- Why can't you just assume some responsibilities? I don't sit at home and wait for you all day just so I can do the dishes you know.
- It's your turn to do the laundry. There's no way I'm doing that this weekend.
- You were closer to the window; you should have drawn the curtain.
- Why did you take my iPod charger to work???
- Why did you take my iPhone charger to work???
- You weren't supposed to buy white bread. White bread gives you cancer.

The fights were pretty spectacular. If you ever want to watch twenty somethings turn into toddlers just make them try and break up with each other without really telling the other person.

After a couple months Romeo gave up. This wasn't working for him. No matter where he turned, it felt like he was trapped. So he decided to pack his bags and say goodbye. Tea watched him leave with a tinge of reluctance. Somewhere in the back of her mind she knew she was letting go of a good thing. But all her senses were telling her that this wasn't right. This wasn't right for the moment, for right now.

And just like that Romeo was gone.

Years later Tea looked back and thought of Romeo.

She tried to lay out those months as a jigsaw puzzle and after a while of staring at it she realized that it was she who was missing from the picture and not Romeo. He was all there. Sniveling, shuffling, dribbling, goodlooking, guffawing, arguing Romeo. All his pieces fit just fine. It was Tea who was too busy calculating and trying to match things and work them out in her head that she lost out on what was real. She was so hooked onto an *ideal* image of Romeo that she didn't want to consider the flawed, beautiful Romeo right in front of her.

This thought didn't make her sad. Instead it made her realize the follies of a preoccupied mind. This is not to say that had she stuck it out with Romeo it would have ended in a terrific story with a life full of adventure and thrill. This is to say that she would never know. She would never find out if she missed out on a rollercoaster ride of a lifetime because she was too busy being presumptuous. But then again, a decision made is a decision made. And I should probably put on a preacher's hat before saying the next line. Looking back and regretting should be your biggest regret (ba doom doom dish).

Tea knew that. So instead of moping about, she chose to take the happy memories from a time past and go about traipsing through her life exactly the way she wanted to. End of story.

The moral of this story is that not every frog you kiss is going to turn into a prince. In fact, the frog that you really want to be prince, will probably just be a frog because, let's face it, how many times are you actually going to bend over, pick up a frog, and kiss it? And if you do manage to do that (gross), what are you, five? That you're going to believe in fairytales?

Second moral of the story: Grow up.

Last moral of the story: The easiest thing to do is to mope and feel sorry for yourself. But it loses its charm and sheen after the first few days, after which you need to gather yourself or have some friends bitchslap sense into you to get you back on your feet. Perfect, wholesome circle.

Fun Fact: Certain frogs secrete toxins through their skin. Go ahead. Kiss one. I dare you.

8

The Big Letdown

THE FIRST BREAK UP. THE BIG LETDOWN. YOUR HEART broken into tiny little pieces. You can't pick it up so you walk away. You can hear your feet walk all over the tiny shards, crushing them a little more. Then you live without it for a while. With a sinking, hollow feeling. Because there's a vacuum where your heart was. The rest of you is pain. Pain that you have never felt before. Pain that you will never feel again. Pain that you cannot feel again.

There is a certain elegance in your first heartbreak that you only realize much later. But at that moment, you get a visceral sense that you will never be the same again, that life is misery. It's a sense of doom that is incomparable and which lasts for what seems like an eternity. And then you get over it.

A bit abrupt? Yeah, I'd think so. But that's how it rolls.

The first time you bungee, is the first time you bungee. The first time you scuba dive, is the first time you scuba dive. The first kiss you get is the first kiss you get. All these are thrilling first experiences. And because of that they will feel that much more heightened. They will feel surreal, they will feel otherworldly, and they will feel fantastic.

If we apply this logic to your first heartbreak, it will definitely be the most debilitating thing you ever feel emotionally. And that is exactly what it is. It's a first. Firsts are supposed to be events that stay with you forever. And the only way it can stay with you forever is by making you feel the most you've ever felt. Good or bad. It's almost like it has an obligation to life. That some rule was written and it has to follow it to the T, otherwise the universe will explode (or something equally dramatic).

Was I crushed by my first heartbreak? That's like asking if bread is the best invention of mankind. Or if neutrinos are passing through our bodies close to the speed of light right now, or if Pomeranians are, in essence, demonic.

Yes I was crushed (and also—death to all Pomeranians). I was crushed to such a degree that I felt that someone had taken a huge slab of lead and placed it on my chest. I felt I couldn't breathe, I felt my knees couldn't prop me up anymore, I felt listless and vague about everything. But all this came in waves after the first two weeks. I kept myself occupied/distracted.

(In ways that I have mentioned in Chapter 6, but most of the time during this period, it was forced. I had to deliberately get myself to do things I liked to keep myself preoccupied constantly.) For the most part, but then a feeling of absolute despair would sweep over me and I would be reduced to all the versions of pain I talked about a little earlier.

There are many options of dealing with a first heartbreak. Enough has been written about it; friends always have a lot to say about it, family too, but you eventually have to choose a path you're most comfortable with. Nine times out of ten that path is wrong, but then you're in a state of vulnerability where every correct suggestion will be shot down with a tomahawk. So resort to permutations and combinations of different techniques.

I'm going to assume that your first heartbreak happens when you're in your teens or early twenties. Which is when you're at your immature best. So the break up is usually dealt with in these following ways:

1. **Crying (howling/bawling/sobbing/weeping)**: This is natural. This has to happen and it usually happens first. Even if you're strong, composed and quiet, crying usually kicks in on the first day. There is nothing to be ashamed of with crying. It's a natural

human impulse that happens after a certain loss or pain. And you've had both. So you're allowed the breakdown. This is usually the most honest bit of crying that you will do in this part of your life, so just go with it. You might even catch yourself crying in front of the mirror and feeling more sorry for yourself than you should and that is also okay. Heartbreak is a bitch. You won't feel much better at the end of it, because this isn't a tantrum you're throwing or a fight you're losing. This is the real deal. So, cry and don't think much about it.

2. **Feeling sorry for yourself:** Now I'm not one to propagate something like feeling sorry for yourself, but after something as earth-shattering as a first heartbreak, one is allowed to wallow in some self pity. I'd give it a maximum period of a week. Any more than that and you're wasting your time.

   Look at the world around you. There are birds flying in the sky, there are cows walking the highways, there are trees breathing out oxygen, sometimes it drizzles in months when it should not, pinecones and flowers are embracing the Fibonacci sequence, and you...you're just sitting there not looking at any of this magical, amazing world. You have a week for the self indulgence and then you need to snap out of it because, trust me, you will regret it later.

3. **Suddenly being fine:** As much as I'm all for being absolutely fine as soon as possible, when it happens suddenly, there is a problem. You can't force normalcy to come back whenever you want. It has to seep in. It has to be a constant thing in your mind, where your brain takes stock of what has happened, grieves, and then moves on. If you force it, it's going to be temporary and it's going to be superficial. It will start to crack slowly, and then in one quick moment, it will crumble. 'Fake easy breezy you' will give way to 'trainwreck you' and we will have gone back three steps.

4. **Partying:** Who needs love when you have discotheques?! Well, that's what this phase usually boils down to. I know, it sounds awful when I put it like that, but it is what it is. Friends insist that you need to 'get out more'. I usually fail to understand this sentiment because they usually start pestering you with this idea a *week* into your break up. Which basically means, a week ago you were doing just fine and getting out as much as a regular person but now in a week, when someone has ripped out

you heart, put it in a blender, then put it in a glass and then thrown it in your face, your friends have decided to do damage control by taking you out to party. Because that will solve all problems.

Pop quiz: How many people have you met who turned around and said, 'Man, I felt so much better after partying six days a week for two months. I didn't even feel like I had a broken heart'? This is a rhetorical pop quiz. I'm not really looking for a specific statistic. But you get my drift.

5. **Drinking:** Drinking doesn't solve anything. There. I said it. Got it out of the way. Treat that line like a disclaimer from me. Now let me get down to brass tacks. Drinking doesn't solve anything but it really helps you forget your current miserable life for a while. So, I'm not saying hit the bottle, and I'm not saying your woes will be taken care of, but usually, typically, mostly, there is drinking involved after a break up. Unless, of course, you're a teetotaler, which is really good. Because drinking gives you liver cirrhosis and stomach ulcers. Maybe you could get high on dairy. Milk and yoghurt when mixed with a lot of sugar, can give you a sugar high which can make your teeth chatter, and that can count as distraction as well. Since I'm trying to be so careful

with this particular subject, why don't I leave it all to your imagination. I don't want impressionable young minds reading this and then find themselves in an AA chapter a year later. I can't have that karma chase me. So here is a drawing of a poppy flower.

6. **Crying after drinking:** This is pretty fantastic. If the floodgates haven't opened yet and if you are still being that person who want to be, stoic in the face of a storm that is ripping your life to bits, a beer will pretty much break you. Your friends who have never seen you cry or breakdown ever, will now be witness to a sniveling, weepy mess formerly known

as you after a lager or an ale has made its way down your gullet.

This is a good thing. It's alright to show your emotions every now and then even if you are an absurdly private person. No one is going to judge you (this is a HUGE lie). But because no one has seen you cry and wail before, this will either amuse them or worry them. If you're going to drink and bawl, chances are you will slur and also not make too much sense, so it might end up being slightly comical. Some close friends will be very concerned because this is not your ordinary behaviour, other not-so-close friends will talk about this for about a week in hushed tones, or worse, through texts. But that is the story of our lives. It's not a new story, so it shouldn't shock us, but nonetheless it does. Now that I'm on the other side of the fence and I see a girl in the bathroom of a nightclub weeping copious tears and slurring, trying to explain something no one can understand, I want to hug her and tell her it's going to be okay (it's actually not, because the next morning she's going to wake up and feel like running into a wall).

Is this a must? Not really. Does this happen always? Not really. Does this help? Not really. Not everything in life has to be constructive. Not everything has to be a means to an end. Some things are done just for the moment, for the instant gratification of momentary respite, without meaning very much before or after. I'll let this phase come under all that. At some point it will get tiresome for you as well, sympathy will wane from friends and then maybe out of sheer boredom you'll snap out of this.

7. **Meeting new people:** Once you've managed to crawl out of the black hole that is the complete annihilation of your former self, and start to take baby steps into normalcy, there comes the amazing phase of meeting new people. You are suddenly meeting up with all those people who you previously thought to be so dull that you'd rather chew your own arm instead of making any conversation with them (some of them at least). Your friends are not enough, you need to meet more people, get out there, have fun. This is actually the most constructive thing you can do. Your other option is staying at home and playing tetris.

   No one is expecting you to find your next big love when you're out meeting new people, but what you will get is a smorgasbord of personalities, interesting conversation, dull conversation, meeting at places that aren't home ground, which will give your mind a lot to munch on. This is also when you realize that your heartbreak wasn't the worst thing that happened to you. There's a lot happening in the world, and as much as you'd want to be the centre of the universe at that moment, it's good to shake things up a bit and shift the centre somewhere else, so you can actually see the bigger picture, which happens to be very bright and colourful.

8. **Crying after meeting new people:** And then suddenly during a moment of weakness, while talking to an almost stranger, with the help of a kind word, you well up, and all the bravery that you had put out there starts to crumble and you are weeping profusely. In front of a stranger. Who doesn't know what he or she has done to make you burst into tears. They stare at you, and you try to explain in the middle of all your sobs, every word is screechy and high pitched. They don't know what to do, so they pat your head awkwardly and tell you everything is going to be okay while looking around nervously to see if anyone is watching.

   Yep! You've become that girl. It's happened. There was nothing you could do to stop it; you did try your best. Maybe you could make a funny story about it in the years to come, but obviously this is not the thought that goes through your mind when you're actually done crying and are trying to figure out ways to fix your mascara that has reached your cheek, making you look like a heroin junkie.

I'm sure everybody has their own experiences to deal with heartbreak, but this is the most typical permutation–combination I could come up with. And maybe this was a linear path of experiences that I followed. Maybe. No one will ever know.

I wish I had a solution for this, for a first heartbreak. Something that would make the pain go away or even a little less, but unfortunately I don't. I don't think anybody does. This is the part where we learn to grow up a little, and for a moment believe in love a little less. But that changes, and that much I can guarantee.

9

Witch

I WASN'T AFRAID OF WITCHES TILL THE TIME I ASKED my mother if she was afraid of ghosts. And she said that she wasn't. Then I asked her if she was afraid of anything at all and she casually mentioned that she didn't like the idea of witches. I didn't get it. I asked her why? To which she replied saying that they (witches) were her one irrational fear. That ghosts, spirits, and witches had been built up with different ideas of fear. She had once watched a movie in which all the witches of a town got together and surrounded a couple in order to kill them. These witches were regular women in the movie until the very end. My mother must have been very young to have had this film affect her in a way that so many years later she was telling her daughter about it.

Now the thing with me is that I get spooked easily; so most things that scare me are borderline children horror stuff. Jump out from behind a wall, say boo, have a friend call me and say 'Don't look under your bed', etc. I don't think I ever let my mind wander far enough to think of the dangers that were lurking in other forms. I was pretty content with my limited Frankenstein meets Casper the Friendly Ghost house of fear. But the more I thought of witches, the more I began to see sense in what my mother had said to me. While the conical hat, long-nosed, broom + cauldron variety of witches doesn't really exist, they do come in other special shapes and sizes. And you don't really realize their existence until, unknowingly, you encounter one. Once you do, they breathe life into your paranoia, your nightmares, lower your self esteem, and leave you feeling worthless. If you still can't see them, here's how you'll know.

- That girl who leans a little closer to your boyfriend while talking to him.
- That girl who looks like what you have always wanted to look like.
- That super confident, hot, intelligent girl who knows everything and everyone and doesn't have a bad bone in her body.
- That silent girl in the corner who is emitting more pheromones than all the girls combined who make up your 'crew'. (P.S. Call it a 'crew' and lose a few pheromones for free.)
- The conniving, insecure, beautiful model/actress who constantly wants all eyes on her because she has no other way of reassuring herself that she is important

and beautiful (not in that order).

- The flirtatious young thing who has just discovered her sexuality and wants to try it out on everything that is not chiefly estrogen.
- The rogue recluse, who has everyone's attention by being absent (spiritually/emotionally, everything except physically).
- The traveler who has more adventures to talk about than Captain Cook and has everyone's rapt attention.
- The scholar who, in spite of having enough intelligence to teach the Mossad a thing or two, is secretly needy and will stop at nothing to get that sliver of attention that was denied to her all through her years of tuition and eating books.

Have I missed out any category? I should think not. This is a broad spectrum of what would make up a witch. For you. At some point in your life. You want to know how? Well, for starters, she wouldn't really have to do much to you per say, but just to the object of your affection. Sometimes, it doesn't even take words.

We've all dealt with jealousy at some point in our lives. It's not fun. In fact, it's the most un-fun you can have in a relationship. How then do you deal with it? If it's the sort of jealously that you have made up in your head, then there is only one solution. You.

To me, there is nothing sexier than a confident woman. A woman comfortable in her shoes, whether they be 5-inch high heels or worn out rubber soled canvas shoes. A woman aware of her sense of being, of her individuality, a woman not trying too hard, and wearing her skin like she belongs in it. Because she does. After all, at the end of the day, we all notice people and things that aren't assembly line similar. It's the uniqueness of people that attracts us (that and obscene good looks), and since we're all made different, all we need to do is go with the flow and embrace the person we are or will become.

Unless someone is chasing you with a spoonful of jealousy and trying to pour it down your gullet, you don't have to accept it. You can actually shake it off. Eight times out of ten it's our imagination having a field day. The other two times are when:

- Your partner is saying things/doing things that will make you want to have them lynched or yank all your hair out (painfully). The reason for this could be many, but you need to fix this soon or else, you will be a nervous, anxious wreck. Deliberate jealousy is a cruel joke and not meant to be played on anyone.

- When you're pretty certain that a witch (one of many mentioned earlier) is trying her level best to dismiss the idea of someone else's relationship chiefly because she is scum and secondly, because she has had her EQ carefully extracted from her every pore and has no regard for anything even remotely sacred.

The latter can be dealt with finesse, but as women, we tend to take our time getting around to it. If the witch's party tricks fall flat on her face and she gets zero attention, you're good. There's nothing to worry about. However, if the tricks work, you're good too, because honestly what good is love if it's going to have a roving eye? Now that I've solved one of the trickiest problems of people's love lives, let's go build a utopian city where there is no famine or disease.

Like I said, a lot of this is easier said than done. The older you grow, the more assertive you get, the less insecure you feel, and the witches seem to have taken off on their brooms. Now here's the interesting part. Did you ever think that maybe at some point in your life you played the part of said witch? Knowingly or unknowingly. If I hadn't covered your personality type in the list I made of witches, please feel free to go ahead and add to it. Fact is, at the end of the day, you have been the reason for someone's jealousy, whether you like it or not. It may have happened fleetingly or for a prolonged period of time, but it has happened. If you try and deny this, you better belong to a convent, wear a habit + a paperbag on your head at all times. If not, then take my word for it.

This shouldn't come as a shocker. We would love to think that we are all guileless with a coating of innocence, and I'm sure to some degree we are (that degree being that we are not gun-toting thieves), but we have been that girl who has made someone a little ill just by her presence. So the question begs to be asked, do we burn the witch? Do we tie her up, stack up logs of wood, get some gasoline, and set everything on fire? Yes. If we are lobotomized, 12th century, frock-wearing peasants. No, if we are a notch above 'savage'.

What if jealousy is something we need to tackle ourselves instead of trying to get others to tackle/solve it for us? Why let someone affect you so much that it starts to make you queasy? That every few minutes your thoughts wander away to that person? That it becomes one step short of an obsession? That's not the least bit healthy and we know that, but how do you shake it off?

There is no big answer. No statement that will have a magical solution to rid you of the green-eyed monster or for that matter, even the witch. This is the part where it helps if you know yourself a little, and know yourself with honesty. If you have a tendency to make a big deal out of things, ordinary things, everyday things, then chances are that you may be blowing things out of proportion in your head. You have to be brutally clear about the way things are, make a mental list of the things that bother you, and how real they are.

Are you jealous because you feel that the 'witch' in question is better than you or is the kind of person your lover will be attracted to? Because these are not very solid grounds for jealousy. In fact, in my book, they're pretty lame. These are assumptions you have made because a) you might feel inadequate and b) the feeling of inadequacy leads you to believe that your partner would definitely want this other fantasy creature more than you.

This is also where you need to kick yourself in your shins or have someone else do it for you because you're just giving yourself grief over fiction. Neither of the assumptions you may have made are real at that moment. This is stuff that you have to deal with. Unless you can sort your own mind out, everything will spiral out of control. That already active imagination will spin stories in your head you never even thought possible. Soon it will be you and your imagination with a web of lies. And you will see no logic but continue to believe in these lies unless you snap out of it.

SNAFU.

Stockholm syndrome.

Between you and your imagination.

This is all sounding rather dramatic. I want to take a break and go wear a trench coat for some reason.

Know that you are a wonderful person (unless you're not, in which case, lie to yourself). Tell yourself that there are other more important things to worry about than to be a worry wort about things that are only happening in your mind. Concentrate on work, friends, your lover, go for a jog, eat healthy, wear bright red lipstick and try feeling fabulous, think about Kim Jong Un's girlfriend who got shot in North Korea on his orders. There are other terrible things happening in the world. You and your unfounded jealousy are not in the top ten. It takes seven days to make a habit. Make it a habit not to worry. Because with situations like the one I just talked about, you don't really need to worry.

Then there are other situations. Situations in which we don't make things up in our minds. Situations of jealousy that are warranted, where there are external factors involved. If someone is trying to make you jealous, as childish as this may sound, it would be best to see why. There must be a reason behind the actions. If there are none, then you are dealing with a person who is either very selfish or frivolous. Either way, it would be best to extract yourself from such a situation, even if it is for a while, to see whether or not you're willing to put up with this (it's best to walk away into some sunset rather than walking back into a relationship that is fit for a 13-year-old pre-pubescent teenager).

At the end of the day there are three things you need to keep in mind.

- Jealousy creeps up when you least expect it.
- When you're in the vortex of jealousy, steady yourself and tackle the problem like the rational, evolved adult that you are, instead of losing yourself and becoming a crazed version of you that you never knew existed.
- When you've managed to rid yourself of it, the witch(es) in question seem to vanish into thin air, making you wonder if they were ever there at all.

Fun Fact: The term 'green-eyed monster' was first coined in *Othello*. Shakespeare alludes to cats as green-eyed monsters (because the cat has green eyes) in the way that they play with mice before killing them.

> Iago:
> 'O, beware, my lord, of jealousy;
> It is the green-eyed monster, which doth mock
> The meat it feeds on; that cuckold lives in bliss

Who, certain of his fate, loves not his wronger;
But, O, what damned minutes tells he o'er
Who dotes, yet doubts, suspects, yet strongly loves!'

10

Girls Who Love Boys

TO MAKE MY LIFE EASIER, MOSTLY BECAUSE I AM A LAZY bastard, I decided to ask some women I know the one thing they wished they knew about love.

Some took a while to think about this, whereas some knew exactly what it was.

Here are their answers:

- 'I wish I knew how to stay away from it, or at least keep it in check. I suppose a sense of control over the emotion would be great.'
- 'What is the intensity of love? Can one ever know?'
- 'How honest is one's love? Is there even a measure; rather is there a need for measure?'
- 'I wish I had known how deeply I could love.'
- 'I wish I knew how not to be an obsessive, unbiased "my boyfriend can do no wrong" love-struck idiot.'
- 'How never to get bored of that person. That's massive. I mean, dude, how do you always stay in that level of love?'
- 'I wish I knew why people think you can change

someone because you love them. If you don't respect that person, you can't love them.'

- 'I wish I knew that love is a reminder of what I already know. I wish I could tell my younger self that by looking for love, I will not necessarily find happiness.'
- 'In any relationship, if you aren't happy with the person that you are, then the whole relationship/the couple that you become, will not be happy.'
- 'What is love? Baby don't hurt me, don't hurt me, no more.'
- 'I wish someone had told me that love never ever leaves.'
- 'There are shades of love, each as intense and lasting as the other.'
- 'I wish I knew how to balance head and heart.'
- 'That it goes beyond two people. The idea of "oneness", real actual oneness blows my mind.'
- 'The different levels or definitions of love fascinate me. You've been with someone for years and you can't fall asleep at night without using his arm as a pillow. That comfort level is love. Then there is another case where you've just met someone. They barely know each other but can't get enough of each other. That's love too. How do you know which one is the real deal? It's a convoluted and dumb question.'

- 'I wish I knew that love isn't enough and that love fades away.'
- 'Why is it impossible to love someone just as much as we loved someone else the first time around?'
- 'How is it that love can bring out both the best and worst in someone at the same time?'
- 'That it could be everything you never wanted.'
- 'That it is an alien that controls all you life decisions subconsciously.'
- 'I don't even know what love is. Unless you mean my relationship with wine.'
- 'I wish I knew how long you can stay in love with the same man (not only love him but to stay in love with him).'
- 'How to make someone love you back.'
- 'Once you have it, how can you be sure this is the one, that you should compromise and stop right there?'
- 'Once the love has left the building, how do you get over the person quickly and permanently?'
- 'Why is it so complicated and why does it come so easy?'
- 'That the joy you feel when you're in it and the pain you feel when it's gone are equally transient. So both should be taken with a pinch of salt.'
- 'That it's more about the head than the heart.'
- 'I wouldn't want to know anything. The whole point of falling in love is discovering the person and

realizing why you want to love him/her. To learn new things about them and fall more in love because of it!'

- 'I'd say that love isn't anything without trust. Just because you love someone doesn't necessarily mean you can trust them! The amount of love you give has to be proportional to trust. Because otherwise you just end up hurting yourself.'
- 'Can you love only one person for your entire life?'
- 'Can the person you're in love with satisfy every need that you have from a relationship?'
- 'That you can feel it as deeply for your friend or family as for your partner since it manifests itself so beautifully as you grow up.'
- 'I wish that I knew that it was conditional.'
- 'I wish I had been told how difficult it can be.'
- 'I wish I knew how to get it right.'
- 'I wish I knew how love can make me feel all emotions for this one person!! Love (obviously), anger (when he acts like an arsehole), jealousy (when he throws a tantrum like a child I wish could act the same), hatred to a certain degree when he acts like an arsehole raised to the power of n), joy, satisfaction, pride, attraction, desire, alarm! I could go on and on.'
- 'I wish I knew what it is about love that makes one fall in love.'

- 'I wish I knew why people would compromise on it for material things. It just doesn't add up.'
- 'I wish there was a single universal definition of it, because more often than not, people have skewed opinions of what they have and enough reason to believe that it's true love, when perhaps they have no idea of what true love really is, and the ignorant fools leave no room to accommodate for the possibility of them having made a bad judgment call.'
- 'How long would it last?'
- 'I also wish I knew how to manipulate love. As in, sometimes I have not known how to love someone back, even though I have been loved. It really is the one thing you can't control.'
- 'What would also be interesting to know is the biology of love. How does one love, why does one love and how much can one love? How far would a person go for love?'
- 'I wish I knew that love is a slippery slide with no control.'
- 'Everyone has a past and a future, a good and a bad side, a right and a wrong.'
- 'Love means embracing every little part of the person you're in love with.'
- 'I wish I knew it needs constant work.'
- 'Animals also love, but how can it be compared to

the love humans feel? One sees animals rescuing their babies and scientists call it instinct, but isn't that in fact also love? How much of the love we feel is instinct? Is it all just instinct? Something's go beyond that, like when a lion is a mother to an impala (once reported in Kenya). Maybe something's should not be explained scientifically.'

Forty-six different, yet similar, wishes from women from different age groups, from different walks of life, ranging from my closest friends to my cousins, my mother and friends I have made over the years.

Maybe the point of this entire exercise was for me (and you) to see that not all questions about love are answered, that people around you wonder about the same things that you do, and that at the end of the day all we're trying to do is make love simple. Some of us are lucky enough to figure it out, while others take their time.

I'm going to maintain that love is strange. And strange can be poetic. With that thought in mind, here is something a friend wrote to me recently that makes perfect sense to me and sums up the strangeness of love.

'Years ago I asked my mother what love was. And she said "chemicals". Some people make the chemicals in your body react in a way that feels really good.'

11

Mathematics, Travel, and All That Jazz

IF LOVE ISN'T AN OBSESSION, THEN WHAT IS? IT'S AN all-engulfing act that washes over you like a massive tidal wave. In its presence you breathe, sleep, eat, and rest with love. Have I said this enough times already? Now let me try and equate this with the one thing you thought you did not (cannot) love. Mathematics.

Remember staying up late at night just before your math exam? Remember not being any good at it? Remember thinking that you'd work on it and get better, but never really getting around to it? Remember hoping for a miracle just before walking into the examination hall? Remember those three days before the exam where all you did was spend every waking minute—and there were quite a few because you figured sleep was a waste of time—going through every little piece of your syllabus you had chosen to ignore through the year? Remember sleeping and have equations come flying at you in your dreams? Then there was the queasy feeling the morning of the exam; there would be hints of hypoglycemia, lightheadedness, parched mouth, and cold fingers. All signs of sudden death. Remember looking at the paper and feeling all the breath from your body being sucked out?

No?

Fine! Replace 'mathematics' with the one subject you sucked at.

Bazinga! See what I mean?

Sure it doesn't feel as good as love, but if you take a closer look at all the symptoms, behaviour and nausea, it is a lot like love. I'm going to compare it with milk and soy milk. They're both white, liquid, and go with tea. Except only one of them is the real deal.

Why am I talking about mathematics? Maybe just to let you know that there is a phase in your life when everything ceases to matter except the one thing that you really want to focus on. Now whether you want to focus on it because of desperation or desire is secondary. It is a paradigm shift in your 'love' life. Your basic needs dwindle to the very basic, and your fervour becomes heightened. Food, sleep, friends, the outdoors all become unnecessary. If I had to draw parallels between love and math, I'd probably run out of bullet points. Yes, mathematics and love are similar.

But what do you do with that? How is this bit of information essential for you?

I'll get to that in a bit, but first I must talk about my

most favourite thing in the world that isn't a red velvet cake. Travel.

My entire life has been about travel and new places. I have chosen jobs on the basis of how much I could travel. Pay and benefits be damned. If the job didn't have as much travel, then I needed to make sure I was making enough money to take off whenever I wanted. It's the one thing that has always driven me. Now travel may not mean as much to you as it does to me, but I'm pretty sure you have a well-matched alternative. It could be gardening, parasailing, scuba diving, or welding. It doesn't matter what it is, as long as you have that one thing that when used to describe you goes first up as a mention.

We grow up picking and choosing things that take our fancy and then eventually die out after a while. Traveling remained my constant. There were other things, but if I had to pick one thing to keep forever it would be this. My love for it is endless and nothing gives me the kind of joy a new place or the unknown does. This is essential for having a life well lived, to have something to call your own. To know that if all else fails you have that one safe place to go to and make things better, to know that you will always have this. This facet of your personality takes you a long way, it adds to your intrigue.

What has travel got to do with love?

Well, nothing much with carnal love, unless you're in a long-distance relationship, but travel or any other constant that you may have chosen in your life is a lifelong love. It doesn't come across as a forever/eternal love, but it is what keeps you sane. It makes you more you than you imagine yourself to be. Let me try and explain this better.

I like going to Ladakh. I've been there only thrice, but it's really far away and a bit of an arduous journey. I went there the first time for work and I honestly felt that if magic had a physical appearance or if it could be condensed into a feeling, Ladakh would be it. Meeting a gang of motorcyclists who worshipped Shiva (these guys were Norwegian, Israeli, Japanese, and American), have one of them knit me a scarf, meeting a musician, freezing to death because of inappropriate clothing, breathing air so clean that I felt my lungs would explode, riding up to the highest motorable rode in the world, freezing there as well, and spending the evenings looking up at the stars. It was a picture postcard in motion. I was in love, with a place and a feeling, and I was not going to shake it off. I came back twice, once when I was heartbroken and another time when I was not. But each time I left, I felt whole. I felt light, clean... like my brain was smiling. As creepy as that sounds it's actually a wonderful feeling. It's when every molecule in your body is taking it easy and wearing sunnies.

To be honest, there is no love like what you feel in solitude. And that solitude can be anything. It can be whatever takes you away from the humdrum of everyday life and into a space, which you can call your own. It's a general sense of well being, the exact opposite of anxiety, when you are so comfortable in your skin that whatever worries you might have, are fenced out, to be dealt with later. That is my idea of bliss. That is my idea of love and to be this is the most essential. This is when you have no masks and no ready answers because there's no one around except you.

From travel I want to traverse to music—the other essential love in my life. One of my favourite lines that encapsulates how I feel about music is by Nietzsche. 'Without music, life would be a mistake,' he said. And it really would. It's only been a hundred odd years since music could be recorded and then made portable, prior to that it was live and you had to be of privilege to experience it every day. But it has been one of the core arts, loved at every age, loved by every age, developed to suit every generation, finding its way into our daily lives.

I remember being much younger and aching to feel sad because my hormones were losing their mind, so I would play sad music and immediately get into a funk. It served the purpose. The same can be applied to the opposite. Go to a music festival and feel the energy all around. That brilliant, crystal clear, shining happiness that everybody's face is showing? All music. (Some of it might be drugs, so steer clear of that.) To have the ability to control something that is external, which can tweak your moods, isn't that fantastic? I'm of the belief that if we all had a soundtrack to our lives, life would be several percentages better. Music makes everything better—love, heartbreak, longing, loneliness, travel, inertia, dull people. It's good to be and stay in love with music.

To know that somewhere someone is sitting and stringing notes together to weave a song out of thin air just so you can hear it someday, if that isn't poetry, I don't know what is.

Mathematics, travel, and music. Three things I happen to love with all my heart, somehow interconnected yet at the same time so very distant. All with an underlying fabric of love. One teaches you the symptoms and behavioural aspect of love. The other teaches you a love unlike any other you have felt before—subtle, sublime and simple. And the third made with ample amounts of love.

The act/sense of love is a glorious thing. It's unfortunate that we only relate to it with another person. The many facets of love and adoration can be had without the requirement of another person. Once we learn to understand this and balance it out, love, literally can be, many a glorious thing.

12

Deceit

THIS BOOK IS A COLLABORATIVE EFFORT. AT NO POINT can I take complete credit for it. Tackling a subject like love, which is a trickster to begin with, is not easy. Plus, I don't think anyone is an authority on it, yet paradoxically, everyone is an authority on it. There is no right or wrong. It's usually what works for you. So I've spent quite a few evenings, mornings, phone calls, texts and casual chats starting with 'What do I write about love? What part of love should I tackle?', and I'll have you know my friends and family have been genius idea givers and chapter helpers.

'Deceit' comes from a discussion I had with a friend who insisted that it is always part of an urban relationship. When I quizzed him more about it he said it is that time of the relationship when one partner just isn't sure about being in the relationship anymore, but won't or can't say anything. I was still a bit confused and I asked him how does deceit work its way in? He explained by saying that deceit lies in covering up. Covering up the fact that you no longer want to be with your partner, and trying to mask that feeling with other things. Deceit begins with deceiving yourself.

You become scared of letting go of what you have and are consumed with the fear of falling into an abyss with no return. You cling on to a liaison that you clearly don't want a part of, because in front of you is a long road to loneliness, which you have built yourself. It is an imaginary road; you just end up making it real with every single thought (Ref: Chapter 1. Old cat lady on rocking chair with your face).

So armed with this you stay in a relationship that is not happy and you seek out some kind of satisfaction from someone new. And in this golden age of technology which gives us the devious pleasure of living in the real as well as virtual world simultaneously, our lack of surety makes us seek out something more, something better, something that we can use in place of what we already have. That one-foot-out-the-door is a form of deception. That constant lookout for a better mate even when you have one standing right next to you.

This becomes easier to do with a spruced up profile on various social portals. Glossy photographs in the angles that make you look good, a very manicured description about your likes and dislikes (Ppl ryting lyk dis dnt gt lucky. Eva), quotes by Rumi and Pablo Neruda making you look like the spiritual lover you aspire to be, kitten/puppy photos generously sprinkled to add to your humane, adorable side. The virtual world is one big Photoshop machine and everyone gets to look good.

And you also get to pick your potential next lover. Scouring, silently stalking, watching—we've all done it. Just because it isn't 'in your face lying or cheating' doesn't mean it isn't borderline deceit. But the question begs to be asked, is it wrong? Or is the way of the world now?

Access to people has become much easier, making social interactions, albeit mostly virtual, effortless. As a girl you no longer have to wait for a guy to ask you for your number. You can casually send him a message on Facebook telling him how bored you are on a lonely Friday night. Slam. Bam. Instead of resolving a problem with a relationship you wrap it up and walk away into the sunset, secretly hoping twitter handle @ ImCool&SexyBoi will meet you half way.

Distractions come easy, so the fatigue of resolving problems seems so cumbersome that to exit and start something new and thrilling has its own sense of excitement, beautifully wrapped in fairy lights and heart-shaped bubbles.

It doesn't start out as deceit, but eventually, and if you allow it, it slowly and softly turns into chicanery. This gives rise to the ability to weasel out of a relationship, instead of giving it the grace that is required to end a relationship.

Having someone in hand before letting go of the first. No one says this is wrong, but if you walk around with a funny feeling in the pit of your stomach thinking you did something wrong, you probably did.

When you chase the idea of love while paying little or no heed to where it comes from, then love stands on shaky ground. It gets passed around and has little to do with finding its roots. It is a choice you make and if you're clear about that choice, then know what it comes with.

Pick a side. I've always believed in this little line. Pick a side, choose a path, and roll with it. Grey areas bore me. There's too much noise and very little said, there's a lot of assumptions and too little done. But then again, that's just me. Some people like treating grey areas like a sandbox, building lofty castles in them. Since I've steered clear of that sandbox there's not much I can say about it, but you should imagine me holding two thumbs up with a big smile and driving away (in a Mustang).

The black and white bits are easy. If you want a steady relationship, then you have to steer as clear of deceit as it may be humanly possible. Because if you're found guilty, you will have hell to pay, and then it won't matter whether your partner is doing the same as you, it just becomes a game of who gets caught first.

If you don't want it steady, don't lie to yourself, because this opens the grand old door to deceit. (Deceit begins with deceiving yourself. I believe I said these fabulous quote worthy golden words earlier at the beginning of this chapter.) Having relationships without being emotionally attached is fine as long as no one is being fooled in the bargain. The trick lies in being on the same page as your partner from the get go. (And try not to be an asshole about it.)

The truth is, everyone lies in a relationship. Tiny little white lies, tiny little bits of untruth that slide into the mundane life of a relationship for no reason or for a big reason with a lot of justification backing them up. The question is—where do you draw the line?

I took a poll to see if people lie in a relationship and why, and most of the people I asked replied with a 'I sometimes lie to get out of an argument', which was chased with a close second of 'I have lied sometimes to not hurt my boyfriend'. As noble as these sentences sound, the questions we really need to ask are:

a) How big would the argument have been had you not lied? Breaking things inside the house kinda bad?? Punching a wall bad? Calling off the relationship bad?

b) How badly would you have hurt your partner had you not lied?
c) Would he have run into a wall? Run far away from you? Alaska far?

Depending on the depth of these answers you will find all your reasoning either crushed to dust or rock solid.

Deceit is for the insecure and deceit can also be universal. The Venn diagram for deceit would be a giant circle because what I just said sounds contradictory. Reiterating, depending on the level of deceit, everyone has had a piece of that pie (I should seriously try another career). Chuck Palahniuk says, 'On a long enough timeline, the survival rate for everyone drops to zero.' Using that as a blueprint for making other drab sentences look cool, I would say that in a long enough relationship, the deceit levels go from zero to definitely.

We've all checked our partner's phones when they've been in the shower, or gone through their Facebook while they've been in the shower, or checked their emails while they've been in the shower (clearly showering is very important for spying on someone). In our technology assisted urban lives it's difficult not to casually go through the many devices/apps/portals that people subscribe to.

This is what I understood from the conversation

with my friend. And after deconstructing it in my head I realized that I might have been deceitful in my life on more than one occasion. I don't consider myself to be a bad person (the range of bad person being: axe murderer to serial killer) but then again, maybe I'm just lying to myself. Do we really live in a world where the absolute and complete purity of a relationship is maintained? I don't know. Everyone I have spoken to has slipped up in the tiniest of ways once or twice. Can we pin it on our curious nature? The need to know, morphing into the need to spy? There is a fine line, and crossing it may lead you further down the rabbit hole, to a place where you had no intention of going, but since you're there you might as well go further.

Deceit may be a small or big part of relationships. As long as it doesn't become the crux of it, it can be manageable. To be aware is key. To know that it's not fair to pry into a person's life and be hurt by what you find. Trust would be easier to live with. Trust until proven otherwise. I feel this would help us to be lighter on our feet and happier in our head.

I've been lucky enough to be surrounded by people who have always had something interesting to say about most things in life (this is probably the most ambiguous statement I have ever written).

Seven years ago a friend said, 'What you don't know

can't hurt you.' I love this philosophy. Life is a little too short to sit with a constant frown thinking about things that may or may not be. I embrace this version of 'ignorance is bliss' philosophy and it keeps me happy.

13

Je Ne Regrette Rien

NOW THAT I'M GROWN UP AND FEEL LIKE A BETTER, MORE patient version of a previous skittish me, I wonder if there were things I could go back in time and fix.

One would definitely be my mid-twenties half shaved head, also my collection of striped tights and man sweatshirts. I'd also like to gift myself a razor. But these frivolities aside, I probably would like to hand out a huge dollop of patience and ease to myself. For some strange reason everyone is absurdly shortsighted while growing up into adults. Life seems like all of it has to happen in the twenties and after that it is just some sort of dark oblivion where one is going to float aimlessly without a cool spacesuit.

I'm well into my thirties and I don't seem to be facing any oblivion. I feel like I am at an age where I have enough patience to have a dance off with a monk, I feel a little more grounded than I did a decade ago and I know that even though I set my twenties on fire, it was necessary to do that for this calm to take over my life. And I like this placid feeling. Of course, there are times that I may nod off at dinners, but that's only because of an iron deficiency. My point is—this is the best I've ever felt and it's because it took a while for all that patience and assurance to trickle in over the years.

When I look back, there are half a dozen things I wish I could change about myself. Would I qualify them under regrets? Maybe not, but I would definitely change them if someone could hand me a time machine and some chloroform.

- **Slamming doors**

  What is that? How does slamming doors help? Who does it make mad? Who does it teach a lesson to?

  I have no real answers for this. I know that that moment of slamming a door can make you feel like a winner, but that is a split second thought. It passes by showing you the middle finger. You are a child. That's your problem.

  I remember this one time I slammed a door and there was a piece of plastic between the door and its frame, and this obstructed the door from slamming and hitting the decibel level I was aiming for. I felt my face turn crimson, I removed that piece of plastic and threw it with a force that could have put it into orbit, and then slammed the door a second time. Really loud. That showed the world. I was superior. I had made my point. Except that I hadn't. In under a minute I felt stupid. Like always.

Dissipating that urge to destroy doors is important. That is the first step to conquering anger...or something like that. Walking away quietly has a certain grace to it. And grace is important. A friend of mine took this a step further. He rose above slamming doors. He kicked a wall. And broke his foot.

I think I need to end this segment here because it is pretty self-explanatory.

- **Hanging up the phone**

This is similar to door slamming but more shameful and humiliating. To yourself.

Let me try to explain this. First the door slamming happens and then you are alone but you can still pick up the pieces and your dignity at some point.

Once you hang up on somebody while they're mid-sentence and you're furious, you know for a fact that nine times out of ten that person is not going to call you back because you are a 'psycho b*tch'. You then wait it out, rationalize, realize, consider calling back immediately, dial the number, hang up, and finally after a couple of hours of stewing in your own humiliation, you pick up the phone and call back. The phone call is long, with you indignantly trying to explain why you behaved like a 4-year-old, with very little steady ground to stand on. This is not fun. At all.

And from personal experience I can tell you that this isn't a 'once bitten, twice shy' situation. I know I didn't learn and I kept at it for years. I have no idea what I was expecting out of it. Maybe my thought was that someday after hanging up the phone on someday, a blanket of bliss and peace would envelope me and angels would play harps in the background. That didn't happen. Not once. And eventually I learned.

- **Jumping to conclusions**

If you have a vivid imagination and slightly above average intelligence, you're doomed. This is not a joke. I'm dead serious. Unless you have used all that imagination and fused it with ample amounts of eccentricity and become Dali, you're pretty much finished when it comes to relationships. Here's why: You will never need to wait for an answer or an explanation because you will have made that up on your own with lots of proof, bolstering the made up reasons.

If you're ever in doubt about a situation in a relationship, in the time it takes you to think of the doubt and inquire about it, you will have managed

to come up with at least a handful of answers for whatever question you have. This is because you are:
a) smart
b) imaginative
c) dumb as a doorknob.

Jumping to conclusions used to be my favourite board game, except there was no board. This was a game I played in my head till I started to go certifiably crazy. I would have to blame it on some sort of superiority I cultivated about being definitely more intelligent than the bourgeoisie. This, of course, caused me a lot of pain, because I would spend a lot of time in my own head working out answers to questions that hadn't even been posed yet. Now what will happen with a situation like this is that once you've rationalized and convinced your brain about a certain solution, the real solution stands no chance to win and upon hearing it your brain starts to break.

It's all very tragic. But this is something one has to learn with time. A soft example of this would be, and this is a platonic friend example, in 2001 my friend Khushnoor was catching a train to come see me. That afternoon there was a mild earthquake in Mumbai. My mother and I were the only ones in our building to run out because, paranoia. And then Khushnoor didn't turn up. She was late by two hours and my brain reasoned with me and convinced me that there was a train collision because of the earthquake and Khushnoor was obviously dead. So when she walked in three hours later (she got busy with work in Pune), I was befuddled. It was a miracle. I was so happy to see her. She had no idea why.

Like I said, this was a soft example. Apply the same logic when your boyfriend doesn't call you back when he's supposed to and his phone is switched off.

Boom!

- **Sulking**

'What's wrong?'
'Nothing.'
'Are you sure?'
'Yes.'
'Okay.'

Two hours later.

'You sure you're okay?'
'Why wouldn't I be?'
'I mean, we've been driving for the last two hours and you haven't said a word to me.'
'…'

'.......'
'WHAT?'
'I DON'T UNDERSTAND WHAT I'VE SAID? WHY ARE YOU UPSET? WHAT'S WRONG?'
'Nothing.'

Isn't sulking grand?

It's an age-old game that is denied by one and all. No sulker has come clean and said he/she sulks. Unless it's one of those women with only a first name who like pink and teddybears and chocolate muffins even when they are 42 years old and have WhatsApp groups called 'girlies'. But those aside, no one walks around a proud sulker. We all know that there is nothing worse than sulking in a relationship. (Okay, maybe I'm exaggerating a bit. Maybe it comes a close second to a violent relationship and cheating, but it's right up there with the bad boys.)

How does one learn to un-sulk then?

I think it's one of those habits that you taper off gradually. You cannot cold turkey sulking. Honestly, that's impossible. You can't wake up one day and decide 'I'm never sulking again' and manage to do it. You'd probably have serious withdrawals and stab yourself in the face just so you could sit and sulk about it. Repressive sulking is the worst, but we're not doing a count off of the kinds of sulking. We're talking about the entire beast that is sulking. Silent, frowning, indifferent, aching for attention but NEVER asking for it.

Wouldn't it be so much simpler to just speak out about what bothers you?

Just say it. Loud and clear. And then, if a fight ensues, at least it is a legit fight. Here it's just you steeped in your own little problem without giving even a mild hint to your partner who is going CRAZY trying to figure out what happened. I'd say that's a tad unfair, but maybe I'm just loco.

I've sulked. For many years. For many things. With many people. It didn't help. Anyone.

If I could go back in time (two years) and thwack myself and say, 'This hasn't worked in the last twenty years. Why are you still at it? How stupid are you?' I would. But I can't. Hence, this chapter.

I weaned myself off sulking. It was a slow process, but I realized subconsciously that I was causing myself a lot of grief. So initially the time of the sulk reduced, then I became picky about the reasons why I sulked, and then I turned into Batman and ruled over Gotham.

But after working on it for a while, today I am a

rare sulker and a much happier person. I do wish I had figured this out earlier because it would have made my life so much easier and I could also have become an emotional coach and made lots of money and bought a boat. I don't have a boat and maybe that is one of my only regrets.

I know I actually said 'half a dozen' things I wish I could change about myself earlier and have only listed four. But that's because a lot of it I have already mentioned in the other chapters. These are childish actions that a lot of adults continue to hold dear and nurture. It's only when you step outside this ring of absurdity do you realize how futile these actions can be. Aside from giving the people around you and in a relationship with you a ton of grief, they solve nothing. And it's a great feeling to shake 'em off and feel rock solid without them.

I know I do.

14

Courting

COURTING. WHAT AN ARCHAIC, BEAUTIFUL WORD. Decades have passed and a good synonym for this word hasn't made its way into our language. 'Dating' is too casual. 'Going around' is too Delhi. 'Wooing' just sounds odd.

Courting. That's where it's at. To be involved with romantically (typically with the intention of marrying). That's the dictionary definition of the word (which was possibly written in a time when courting actually did mean the latter part of the sentence as well).

This is a phase when two people decide to see more of each other because they can't get enough of the other person. Love is, indeed, a splendid thing, especially at this stage.

It all starts with meeting someone you like. You put your best foot forward (because your second best foot is a loser. Just kidding. Both your feet are amazing, but different amazing, so just impress whoever you have to with all your even, pedicured toes). At this stage all your best facets get highlighted. You shower everyday, use perfume, dress up, laugh a lot, and are greeted with a similar version of you in your partner. You take a lot of care, because, let's face it, that is also a definitive side of us. The non-sloppy, non-bed head, non-easy going us. Everyone has a spiffy side and that is the part that is usually highlighted when we're in a courtship with someone (each time I write 'courtship', I take a sip of tea from a delicate china cup and eat a crumpet).

Which brings me to the other side of this coin. I'm sure everyone has heard the 'honeymoon phase' phrase. Much as I detest that term it does sum up six or eight months of the beginning of a relationship with just two words. What with smiles, laughter, chirping birds, sunshine and other postcard worthy visuals, painting a pretty picture of love. If we could maintain our patience, understanding and sartorial sense like we do at this stage, a lot of the frivolous problems of a relationship which crop up later will probably never get nurtured. But then that is rarely the case. Keeping up your best side can be taxing, and with time you start to take it easy, or rather you start to oscillate between your best side and your easy going (with bouts of impatience) side. And this is where trouble kicks in.

The expectations of a courtship are what need to be shot square in the face. If one could realize that the coming months/years are not exactly going to be as rosy as the first six months, things would get a lot easier. That first disappointment, that first sign of irritation in his voice, the first slamming of the door, the first bout of wailing is a gateway to normalcy more than anything else.

And normal isn't all that bad. This just goes to show that you and your partner have a different side to yourselves and the bizarrely happy, Stepford-wife-content masks are finally off your faces. This is actually a good thing.

This could also be a generalization in my own head. So to get a clearer picture I asked a few of my friends whether they changed definitively from the initial phase of the relationship to the more comfortable, knowing-the-other-person-inside-out phase.

'Sadly yes. Most times you don't live with the person in the first six months and you see each other on and off, so yes you make an extra special effort to look nice whenever you meet. Once you start living together that goes out the window, as you become more comfortable with each other. For example, you wake up next to each other and the need to pop a breath mint goes out the door (which a lot of people do before a date).

'However once people get married, the dress up bit, while diluted, still remains on special occasions to remind the other I'm still here, and I'm still sexy. Some things are also taken for granted (and this is not necessarily a bad thing) as one becomes more comfortable you let your guard down.'

This was from one of my friends who has been married for the last two years to the man of her dreams. And truer words could not have been spoken. Love has the ability to take on different shapes and sizes. What is considered love initially morphs into something else later. How you love someone changes as well. It either gets deeper or whittles away depending on the commitment and compatibility of the relationship.

I sound like a relationship scientist with all these big words being strung into one sentence, but as my friend mentioned, habits and behavioural patterns change with time. The trick lies in accepting them, rather than fighting them. Fights are going to happen, the Budhha-like approach to things doesn't always work.

You also get used to the other person and the novelty eventually fades. This shouldn't come as a big surprise. The expectations of the first six months can't be kept up and there can't be constant excitement. To want for that would be unfair. And this I can say from personal experience.

A younger me constantly ached for excitement, probably more than others. Attention deficit may not have been a biological problem with me, but more a spatially ingrained one. It's not normal to change ten schools, seven cities and twenty-seven houses in a span of fifteen years. When that happens, there is some kind of excitement lurking everywhere and you never even have to look for it. Which is why when the excitement left a relationship, usually I did too. It took a while to process this and after years of trying to wrap my head around it and learning how to live in one area code and hold a job down for eight years, did I realize the real meaning of stability and the slight boredom that comes with it.

It wasn't all that bad. It took a little getting used to, but after that it felt good. There was no dire need to slay dragons constantly. This got applied to my relationships as well and not just the ones I was romantically involved in. I suddenly had friends that dated more than two years. I even learnt to fight with them because of the kind of time I was spending with them. Not just passive-aggressive fights, but fights like those with my younger brother. It made me realize that these were signs of a healthy environment. The more time you spend with a person, a place, a job, the normalcy of it all gives way to some mild trouble every now and then, but most of it can be solved. I also feel that the excitement gets split up. It doesn't come in a tidal wave but in short bursts every now and then. And that being with someone for a long period of time does not mean that it was going to be a fairytale every second of the way.

Another beautiful insight came from a woman I look up to. She's beautiful, super smart, and in a very comfortable space in her marriage (she married a man she dated for years). This is what she had to say:

'The first six months of my relationships have been different every time, but it's usually spent fretting over something. One time it was: "What the hell am I doing with him? He's a FRIEND! We're going to ruin our friendship." (I was right. We did ruin it.) Another time it was: "Am I just in it because I'm bored and lonely? I'm not really even that into him." (I was really bored and lonely and he was great but he was just away all the time.) Then another time it was: "I am so madly deeply in love with this guy but I'm still technically seeing this other guy. What the hell do I do?" So like I said, it was all about fretting.

'Now let me come to the ones that were serious. I DID put that person on a pedestal. I thought he was the best guy in the world. Only later did I realize that he wasn't superhuman. He was a regular guy. Also, HE didn't think I was the goddess he thought I was. It was a good reality check both ways. Also, it was a lot more passionate sexually. The first few months are also about trying to figure the person out in every way possible and physical intimacy plays a huge part in that. It's a surge of attraction, curiosity, and hormones. And that of course starts to wane after a while.

'In the first few months, you want to impress the other person and for me, more than clothes or the way I look, it was about trying to sound smart and funny. Of course, after you settle into a relationship, you can ask him the dumbest questions without batting an eyelid. I can also trump him with my smartness when I need to, without trying too hard. The guy I'm with has never affected the way I dress. I wouldn't say I made more of an effort, mostly because they haven't been the type to care. My wardrobe choices have been more influenced by my work or my girlfriends.

'I am more patient than others. I pick my battles. I know what the sore spots are and I try not to go there unless I really need to. I hate drama so I just try and look past it (not before seething and getting a few ulcers or venting to a girlfriend first).'

There's a lot of insight in these last few paragraphs. From the shy, slightly awkward phase, to passion, to discovery, to the various changes you go through when in a relationship, it has been encapsulated in one fell swoop.

I will have to agree vehemently about the excitement

waning, but at the same time I feel that it doesn't just wane. It's like taking the surge of excitement you feel constantly during the 'honeymoon period' or the time you spent in 'courtship' (tea and a crumpet) and breaking it up into tiny fragments and getting doses of that every now and then.

Doesn't sound all that bad does it?

That's because it isn't. That giddy feeling keeps coming back. Try taking a holiday alone and then come back to your boyfriend of five years. Let's talk excitement then. To sum this up I have three words.

Roll with it.

Don't hold onto preconceived notions about a relationship. Don't expect it to be a million things. Just roll with it. Whether it works out or not, it'll be way less grief if you let go of your rose tinted glasses and get some real sunshine on your face.

15

Let's Talk About Sex

OR LET'S NOT.

I'm happier to pretend sex doesn't need to be addressed. Much like everyone else in this country.

It's been sixteen weeks and fifteen chapters and I haven't been able to bring myself to write about it. First loves and big letdowns, bad boys and mathematics, witches, Romeos, even unicorns...all done, no problem. Sex? It's the last chapter I'm writing (whether or not it will actually end up being the last chapter of this book remains to be seen).

I'm a private person. I don't want to discuss my sex life with anyone because I don't want to discuss my sex life with anyone. Also because my mother and my fiancé are going to be reading this book. This is the only thing that could get more awkward than my hair stylist giving me a mushroom cut at age 15, two weeks before I got braces on my teeth and about a decade before I could finally swap my Mickey Mouse training bra for one made specifically for non-fictional breasts.

I blame our country. It's been said a gazillion times

before, but I cannot for the life of me understand why a country with a population of 1.2 billion people and bragging rights to the Kamasutra still fools itself into thinking it's all happening through immaculate conception. You'd think the idea of sex is rather skewed in India. The truth is that it's never really talked about. Ever.

Parents avoid the 'birds & bees' talk altogether, and by the time schools get around to sex education, it's been at least a couple of years since your own personal experiments started. All you've got to go on till then is your Biology class, when the forbidden pages of the chapter on the Reproductive System start to turn. This may not be the case today as schools may have wisened up to the fact that the old school format of sex-ed that existed during my school days (in the Paleolithic era) needed to be spruced up. With diagrams of ovaries and testicles which look like different animal heads. I used to draw horns on them. This wasn't about sex for pleasure. This was about sex to make babies. We were given technical instructions and lectures on how a sperm and an egg got together and formed a zygote. That's a buzzkill if there ever was one.

At home, your parents would rather tell you that you were adopted than admit having done the nasty with each other. Which is frankly, a relief, because imagine...

no, don't. Don't ever want to imagine.

In the movies...well, we really have no idea because if it isn't hidden behind two colliding flowers or a flickering candle, our discerning censor boards cut it clean out, so there are no clues there.

That leaves us with the internet to get a better understanding of sex, since nobody I've met in the last five years seems to have read an actual book about this kind of thing. The internet is probably the worst place to learn about sex because it's not real, unlike the chances of your parents walking in on you just as everyone—if you're usually on the wrong side of Murphy's Law, possibly even you—is writhing in pleasure.

Sex is not what the internet tells you. Sex is a private, beautiful act where two people are naked in more ways than one.

I think I was hesitant and unsure to write about sex in a relationship because I didn't know whom I might inadvertently be influencing and how. Are 16-year-old girls going to read this book? What about 14-year-old boys? Could someone misunderstand anything I say? Will it make them never want to have sex? Will it make them want to do it all over the place?

Since these questions were floating in my head with no clear answers, I wondered what I would tell a 14- or 16-year-old me about sex if I could meet her face to face? (First of all, I'd freak out and scream for a while and then after recovering I'd punch her, to see if it hurts me. Space time, you trippy beast.)

Here are a few things I would tell a young me (or a young you if you're as old as me and reading this):

1. 'Sex is not a bad thing'

You may not see any billboards that scream 'sex sucks', but unfortunately our first encounter with sex or even the idea of it, is generally met with disapproval of some sort. It's wrong, it's dirty, it's not something you should be doing. But the truth is, it is something you will be doing eventually. Boys and girls, or boys and boys, or girls and girls will be attracted to each other and one day you will wonder what sometimes follows after holding hands. Some of you sooner, some later.

Don't be in a hurry. No matter what your raging hormones or your friends with raging hormones say, this is not a race. Not one of you is thinking straight. You're thinking dirty thoughts—about a boy or girl in your class, or some really average boy band member from your latest poster. You will spend days dreaming about them, and that's perfectly natural and okay. Sex is not a bad thing.

But it comes with great responsibility.

If you're old enough to have sex, you're also old enough to contract infections that will either make your nether regions itch unbearably, or look so weird you'll want to stab your own eyeballs out.

If you're old enough to have sex, you're also old enough to get pregnant—and if you step outside of yourself for a single minute to look at how you have behaved your entire life so far, you'll realize immediately that parenting is no fun. And you can either study to pass your exams and get school over and done with or you can be running around trying to find good deals on baby diapers (they're surprisingly expensive).

I'm not trying to scare you (me?); I'm trying to tell you why it's important to befriend condoms, to have safe sex, and to remove that poster of the Jonas Brothers from your bedroom wall.

2. The first time is not always the best

True story. I even checked with all my friends, in case it was just me that had gotten off to a bad start. And I got a hundred percent positive response.

We would all like to believe that we are natural born pleasure givers, but honestly, that's just an incorrect sentence. Nobody is born a love machine. Unless you're James Hunt. In which case, hi what's your number?

If you're expecting fireworks and a 9-piece orchestra to play 'Behind the Door' by Nobuo Uematsu, let's just pop that bubble immediately. It will most definitely be something you remember for the rest of your life because:

a) WOW YOU LOST YOUR VIRGINITY, THAT'S AMAZING
b) It might be, in all probability, a lot awkward. And an awkward sexual experience is something that your scumbag brain will remember even after you die.

Don't be disappointed. Things can only look up from here, the awkwardness will fade, and you will thoroughly enjoy being a dolphin one day (see Point 3).

3. Sex is not just about making babies

You already know this. Now go and share this little nugget with all the people who make up our country. Most times you can tell how often a couple has had sex by the number of children they have.

9 children, all 10 months apart = 9 times sexy time!

Be a dolphin, have sex for pleasure, lots of it. One day you will be old and wrinkly. Your hormones would have left the building, giving you hot flashes, and Antonio Banderas will mean nothing to you. NOTHING. Fear that day, and have a happy, sexy life.

4. Foreplay

Do not be with anyone who doesn't believe in foreplay.

I want to leave that line by itself so that you soak it in. I cannot stress more on this point. Life is too short and we are too evolved a species to believe in 'wham bam thank you mam/sir' as a normal way of life.

Anticipation is key, especially when you know what waits for you at that at the end of it. Even google is all for foreplay (well, sort of). Take a look.

Need I say more?

5. Confidante

It's essential to have a friend in your life who you can trust a hundred percent. The sort of friend who doesn't walk around spilling your secrets. And it's even better to have this friend around when you're stepping into the world of sex as an adult (or as someone who might have the potential to be an adult. Since you can't really run to your mother or older sibling for help with sentences that begin with 'When I was naked and getting it on with...'

it's best to have that confidante/friend handy. You might get some terrible advice depending upon their expertise level in the subject, but with regards to getting things off your chest, this is the best bet.

I've never been one to share girly secrets and I've always kept my personal life a bit too personal, but my other friends who are normal say that having that one friend for all those confusing questions and sharing secrets helped their lives in ways that they cannot count.

I could go on, but I don't want to ruin the fun of self-discovery and making your own mistakes—that'll teach you more than any teacher/movie/friend/website in the world. Unless you're subscribed to magazines like *Cosmopolitan*—then your own experience is competing with a quiz on every third page that claims to discover for you your sexual compatibility with your partner, how good you are in bed, what zodiac your partner should be. Enjoy this hogwash too, it's how you fill your time between orgasms in real life.

16

Bullseye

IT WAS 1986. THESE WERE THE GOLDEN TIMES OF VHS tapes and 6-year-old girls having chanced upon Michael Jackson videos. This was also the time when MTV was a phenomenon that existed beyond the shores of India. But contraband has a way of seeping into society like molasses through jute. And because of that our lives were enriched, in spurts, consistently.

It was around this time that I had decided that my one true love was Michael Jackson. He was good looking, he could sing well enough, and his dancing was divine. My mother's younger sister, Rashmi, was my one grown up friend. She would treat me like an adult and was all for breaking some rules here and there. Also, she had amazing hair, which I wanted when I grew up. Rashmi may have noticed my eternal love for MJ, because one day, when I thought my parents were out of the house, I played a MJ VHS tape and danced unabashedly to 'Beat It'. She walked into the room and caught me mid-dance. She asked me if I loved MJ, I replied in the affirmative. Rashmi then proceeded to tell me that she would phone him and tell him that he needed to stop ageing so that in a few years I could catch up with him so that he and I could get married. Obviously I believed her. Why would I not? She was a grown up. She was cool. Cool grownups could do these things. So I waited.

It was 1994. Michael Jackson got married to Lisa Marie Presley.

And broke my heart. I was 14. By now I had realized that Rashmi had only humored a smitten 6-year-old. MJ wasn't waiting for me in some corner of the world with a beating heart on his sleeve (though he had taken her advice on the non ageing bit). In spite of knowing all this, a part of my brain that still retained the feelings of eight years ago was hurt. I had always thought that he was 'the one'. And now look what he had gone and done.

After feeling rejected for a good twenty-four hours I'm pretty certain I went back to daydreaming about someone in my class who was the reason I would go to school everyday.

If I had been so certain that he was 'the one' for me, then how did that change?

(This might sound a little bit dramatic, but then what's the point of life if we don't amp it up a bit?) How did I move on from my absolute devotion to MJ when I was a 6-year-old? I recovered, naturally. Plus the Backstreet Boys had taken over the scene and my hormones. MJ was a love from another time. But The feeling was similar, familiar. Did I chance upon someone and feel clutched in the arms of a one true love? Yes. A few times. In snatches. What can I say, I am a hopeless romantic.

I was having dinner with a friend, and after reaching a semi-comatose state because of too many dim sums and mindless chatter about the promiscuity of our generation (every generation honestly. I have realized that we glorify the past and shroud it in piousness more than we should. The 1960s had Woodstock as proof of this, and then we have the decade that gave birth to sexual promiscuity—the 1920s) just before ordering an egg soufflé bun, I randomly asked him: 'Do you believe in the idea that there is one person for everyone?'

'Yes,' He replied even before I had finished my question, almost as if he had read my mind.

'I said yes before you finished your question. That's how sure I am of this.'

I sat there looking at him for a minute. This is a man who is logical to the point of frustration and here he was saying something most people would refute. We didn't continue the conversation because there was a beauty in everything that had been said and a lot in what was unsaid. He had stated what he innately believed in, and neither he nor I needed an explanation.

I didn't need any convincing. I have been of this belief from the very beginning.

This is what happens when you come from parents (who come from parents) who have been in love with each other their whole lives and have had a lot of fun along the way. It is all you know. So you look for it constantly. Behind closed doors, under rocks, with boys completely undeserving of your love and adoration. And not everybody lucks out immediately.

This however begs the question—how do you know that the person standing in front of you is actually your lobster/penguin/otter (they hold hands while going downstream and deserve a mention)?

The thing is, when the real deal hits you in the face, then you just know. It's not one action, it's not a statement, it is your brain and all your senses going visceral and know-it-all on you. It is a sense of calm that finds place in the centre of your body while the rest of you is shaking with excitement.

This visceral awareness could definitely be one way of knowing, and as for the others, I did what I think this book needs best. Examples from people who have found love, and contrary to jaded belief, seem rather happy in it.

'That's the funny part about love and knowing he's the one. You don't know entirely when you're starting out but something tells you this feels right, and then you grow together and the experiences you go through make love take on another meaning, more than the adrenaline rush and "I-never-want-to-be-away-from-this-man" feeling you get in the beginning. To be honest no one's perfect, just knowing that and working around it is part of the fun.'

Talk about summing up an abstract thought! This was my best friend of many years saying it exactly like how it is.

We've all had our crushes and people we've lusted after. Sometimes it all rolls up and adds up to who you're in love with and want to be with for a long time. And in no way am I trying to quantify 'a long time'. This could be anywhere from a year to forty-five years. That's entirely your prerogative. Whatever the case may be, it's essential to know about the imperfections that are a part of the relationship.

Here's an example of another way of knowing, though I must add, none of these examples will actually be identical to yours. Every relationship is unique, but this next person wrote back and made me bust out a smile.

'I've never had so much fun in any other relationship. With any other boy, I was always inviting other people to our plans—even if it was a movie or a night out. I don't know if it was because I didn't want to be with them. But I always needed people around because I'd get bored easily. But now, I can spend the whole day alone with him and I'm fine. We have so much fun together. You know all those stupid *Sex and the City*/girl power movies and shows that say: Why do you need a boy? All you need is a best friend? Well, he has become one of my best friends.

'Also, we have this weird thing where we randomly say the exact same thing at the same time. Not regular things. But weird things. I love that.'

How absolutely wonderful to have that, right? I'm actually smiling while typing this. What I do know about the girl who wrote this to me is that she is patient and forgiving, and wise beyond her years. I think that is why she can deal with her relationship with such ease and maturity. Nothing is as effortless as it seems, but sometimes the right people strike a chord and like the sound of what they hear and stick it out. To me, that is the universe making music. And there is nothing more serendipitous and beautiful in the whole world.

Everyone probably has their moment of knowing, whether its gradual, a long time coming, or instantaneous. But what you cannot do is force the moment. I once had someone say two words to me that I will never forget.

'Don't settle.'

Two words that have brought clarity to several situations that have confused me in the past. It is that simple. Settling is so...average and easy. Sure, easy can be fun, but easy also leads to boredom. Not settling means being sure of what you want and sticking by it. It could be a job, the sort of person you want to be with, decisions involving everyday things. Not settling means being passionate. Not settling means being unhappy with second best.

To settle would be to never know that Bullseye moment. Being coaxed (by your own self) into a situation you're not entirely invested in is not fair. To either party. Let me elucidate this with what another friend had to say when I asked her how she knew that her boyfriend was the one.

'I did think at times in my past that my ex boyfriends were "the one", but I'm also of the opinion that sometimes just trying to make something work when the relationship is dead has no point! I'm so glad I didn't hang on because today I know what qualities I would want in my husband and more importantly, the father of my children. With age comes maturity and I'm so glad I wasn't hasty about it! My husband is not a boy, he's a man! He's smart, intelligent, witty, caring, chivalrous, helpful, understanding, loving, positive, patient, handsome, trustworthy, adventurous, and a lover of travel. I could go on and on. He has all the qualities I had dreamed my husband would have. And I sort of knew he was the one when I got to know him instantly. I know this sounds a bit clichéd but there was a little voice inside me that said, "God did send me my prince." It was all matter of time after that, and he turned out to be exactly how I thought he would be. Actually maybe even better.'

There's a lot of love and beauty in this chapter. Mostly because I've chosen to write about people who struck gold and lucked out. There is a flipside to this as well. The times when it doesn't work out. When only one partner feels in love without having it reciprocated. Which then spirals them into a needy state, believing that he/she is the one, but in reality that is not the case. It's not a two-way feeling. Then comes the kick of the jilt, which is as much fun as having your nails pulled out. Clarity is essential, and we all know that nine times out of ten love isn't the best playground for clarity, but the pursuit of that is crucial.

Feeling safe and feeling loved are great signs of reaching that clarity. Stress and anxiety are great signs as well. It's just that they point in different directions.

Michael Jackson ended up giving me stress and

anxiety and in retrospect that's when I knew that we wouldn't work out. I could say the same for some of my past relationships, which is why I bowed out of them gracefully (in some, there was a bit of kicking, screaming, and stabbing but let's not get into the details). Sometimes you just have a subliminal smile pasted on your face on really rough days, and all the effort you put into a relationship seems completely worth it. So this chapter is dedicated to days like that and people who make you feel like that. Dragon-slayer, lover, break-dancer.

17

Wedlock

IS MARRIAGE IMPORTANT?

Age 4: Yes! I want to marry my mother and one very cute boy who came to my birthday party.

Age 8: I really want to marry one of the boys in my class, when I grow up.

Age 12: No! I hate all boys (I didn't really hate many boys. I liked many of them but I couldn't let any of them in on this. Also the idea of marriage sucked then.)

Age 18: No! Not immediately in any case. I'm 18. A child. With bad hair and teeth. And completely hirsute (it's a miracle I didn't get shot while running around in Assam).

Age 22: No! There is no way I am ever getting married. Marriage is an overrated institution for average people. I am not average.

Age 25: No! Life is too much fun. Who in their right minds would ever want to get married? It's all about having a fun job, doing fun things, hanging with fun people, and partying. Clearly, all my friends getting married now are losers.

Age 27: Not really. I mean, I would consider it if the right man came along. But what are the chances of that happening? Plus, men are assholes.

Age 29: At some point sure. Some of my married friends seem very happy, but they are lucky to have found each other. I am a difficult person to be with and my mercurial temperament isn't winning me any brownie points with anyone.

Age 30: OH MY GOD I'M 30!!!!! Does this mean I will have to get married soon? I don't want to get married. Really, I don't. Why am I 30? Old people are 30. I should start working out.

Age 32: I don't think marriage is important per say, but I'm with the right guy, and he is crazy amounts of fun and he really likes me for everything that I am and I'm constantly happy with him in my life. So, if he asks me to marry him, what would I say?

This has been my tryst with marriage so far. Pretty legit if you ask me. Also, a graph typical to all those girls who don't necessarily like the colour pink out of peer pressure and who never obsessed about husbands and babies their entire lives. My take on marriage is very liberal and open minded. If it works for you, great! And if it doesn't, then great too!

There's a lot of societal pressure on getting married at

a certain time/age. And most of it might have scientific backing. Women have a window for reproduction (but recent studies show the window to be broader than narrower)—you don't want to be too old when you have your babies, the chances of meeting someone become less as you get older, etc. As much steam as these statements have, I have never bought into any of them. To me, life is not a series of calculations carried out with surgical precision. I didn't feel that I had to do something because I had reached the age of 24/32/56. It has always been more organic than that. This is the reason why I always had an oscillating take on marriage.

That aside, there are other reasons why one can be sitting on the fence about marriage not being the be all and end all of a stage in life (or life itself). Companionship, on the other hand, trumps everything. Whether it comes in the shape of a husband, lover, multiple lovers, wife, or best friend. Whichever one of these (and any outside of these few mentioned) you pick is entirely up to you. As much as someone may like being alone, we know for a fact that complete isolation calls for a straitjacket and a padded room eventually.

So coming back to the question again, is marriage essential?

Not really. It's a piece of paper that solemnizes the act of aching to be with each other and most times it makes your family happy.

Is it necessary?

Not at all.

Is it worth it?

Sure.

Getting married is serious business. If you're all for it, then you should do it once and for all the right reasons. A person can have several reasons or ideas about why he or she should get married. Now I know I am no messiah of marriage and have zero understanding of it and neither am I married, but after being around a family of successfully married and happy people I have been able to deduce a few things which make perfect sense to me. (You may or may not agree with all of them. Like I said, this is my take so far.)

There are ten broad don'ts and they're self-explanatory.

- Don't do it because it is time.
- Don't do it because she/he has lots of money.
- Don't do it because all your friends are doing it.
- Don't do it because people in your family think you're a hag.
- Don't do it because you are bored.
- Don't do it because you've become absurdly dependent on her/him.

- Don't do it because you want a break.
- Don't do it because you want a big ring.
- Don't do it because you are dying to have a baby.
- Don't do it because your life seems like it's flat-lining and getting married might stir things up a bit and make it exciting.

Here are the real reasons why you should take that life-altering plunge.

- Do it because you both are crazy about each other, and not just crazy (clinically) individually.
- Do it because it doesn't matter if you get married or not. Choose it, together, with dollops of excitement (I want to cite those reasons which I mentioned above again).
- You know the other person's bad side and you're more than willing and ready to tackle it till death do you apart (or aliens abduct one of you).
- Do it because everyone else pales in comparison. The person in front of you is the most exciting creature you have ever come across. (Excitement varies from person to person so this is very subjective. He/she doesn't necessarily have to come with a rollercoaster attached.)
- You've spent enough time thinking how forever

would feel like with this person, and from where you're standing, it seems perfect.

- You've had your share of dull days with this person and they've been exactly that, dull. But you still want more.
- Do it because you have made adjustments to who you are so that there's more compatibility but at no point did you lose yourself (cue Eminem).
- You're the best version of yourself when you're with this person.
- You're happy. Even on days that promise to suck your soul out and send it to someplace dark with ooze, you have a mild current of happiness running through your veins.

I spent enough time scoffing at friends who got married in their early/mid-twenties. It seemed crazy to me. I could see my whole life in front of me with so many things to do, so many mountains to climb, seas to swim, dragons to slay, dandelions to blow, shells to make, stars to gaze at (I should stop). I couldn't for the life of me understand why some people wanted to let go of all these wondrous things and swap them for domestication, to buy cutlery and crockery. I didn't want to hear their side of the story because I knew I'd laugh at it and not believe a word.

That is the folly of youth.

You assign yourself a degree of self-importance that is rather skewed, a bloated sense of self and self-righteousness. In my blinding need to overlook another person's point of view, I forgot that people might want things different from what I do. My way wasn't the only way; everybody didn't necessarily have to think like me. There were people all around me, making decisions and not being struck by lightning. That should have counted for something and percolated down to some sort of understanding in my own head. It did, but it took its own sweet time.

I see now that it is all about different folks and different strokes. Marriage is the most personal of institutions. You should know in your gut what you feel about it and how you want to tackle it. No one can or should give you any advice, which is why I will bring this chapter to an end, but before I do that, I want to share with you a quote from one of the great Greek tragedians, Aeschylus, who sums it up in ten perfect words:

'When a match has equal partners, then I fear not.'

18

Love

AIM FOR LOVE.

Always aim for love.
Let the rest be noise.

This is something that i never needed to be told. possibly because I grew up in an environment where everybody had been aiming for love for generations, so I didn't know another way. My grandfather was in medical school when he met my grandmother. She was two years his senior and very serious about her studies and becoming a doctor. He was very serious about his studies and falling in love with her. I don't think she wanted any of it because of all the responsibilities she had. He didn't care about that because he was in love with her. After a few years she realized that she was too. They got married, had three children, doctored around India while managing a large family and continued to love each other silently. He liked to cook and she never entered the kitchen. They were perfect for each other.

Then came my parents and much as I want to wax

poetic about them, I think it might require me to write another book entirely, so you're just going to have to take my word for it. I learnt all I know about love and loyalty from them (as do most of us who luck out)

It's a bad enough world with enough terrible things happening. If there is one thing right and pure in your life, let it be love. What happens with love is that if you believe in it and if you want it to last, then you have to do it right. You have to get a very fine strainer with a mesh so closely knitted together that you can't even see through. And through this strainer you have to pour in your general idea of love, which can be laced with many things. Someone tall, someone rich, someone very handsome, someone exceptionally brilliant, someone successful and whatever else it is that you have in your mind. You then have to take all these adjectives and make sure they don't get to the other side of the mesh. What you get at the bottom then is a version of pure, unadulterated love. And that's what you roll with. You take that and you build on that. Nine times out of ten you won't need to build anything because a whole brilliant world full of adventure will already await you.

I say this with confidence and no scientific backing. You don't need any of those qualifiers to fall in love. You basically need to go with your gut. No one is handing out guarantees that it will work out just as you planned it either way, but at least you will know you did it right.

Fall in love for the sake of conversation.

Fall in love because you can be silly with each other.

Fall in love because you like his mind more than anything else in the whole world.

Fall in love because he oozes confidence that takes your breath away.

Fall in love because you both like books/travel/sport/food/furry animals/cars/bikes/Edgar Allan Poe/Banksy/surfing/Tenacious D.

Fall in love on a balmy day/winters night/summer afternoon.

Don't plan falling in love.

Don't question falling in love.

Don't change your mind because you fell in love and realized that the person was short on your pre-decided parameters.

Be reckless and not calculated.

Don't think about the future too much. You have today. Focus on today. Tackle tomorrow when you get to it.

Imagine that there's going to be a nuclear holocaust. Once the initial wave of terror of this thought leaves your mind, think of who you would want to be with when that large mushroom cloud blooms over ground zero. That's the person you love.

Don't be jaded because someone broke your heart. This is easier said than done. Realize that you have or will break someone's heart. Such is life.

Love isn't a game. No matter what anyone tells you. A lot of things in life are games, but love backed out of that competition at the starting line. Throw away your dice.

Love is more like origami. Pretty blank piece of paper. Go, fold.

Maybe it has been that much easier for me because I have always had a problem with easygoing, smooth sailing paths. At some point, the fun fades away and things start to get really boring. If everything is paved with smooth, gold bricks and you're moving at a comfortable speed, how will you even know you're moving? How will you realize that you're covering ground when you don't even feel a bump or a jolt?

Isn't adventure all about the unknown? About ups and downs? About shaken and stirred and not blended and smooth?

My favourite memories, even when you take a love interest out of the equation, have been when things have been unplanned. When I've gone on a journey with my parents or my brother or my boyfriend and not had a set agenda. I've slept on the footpath, gone hungry, been in a hot, non air-conditioned car in the peak of summer, traveled by bus, plane, train, trucks, train engines, ran out of money, lost my passport, lost my tickets. These are the journeys that have become ingrained in my memory. The other not so manic ones are exactly that, not so manic. To have your scooter break down during a torrential thunderstorm in Bali at the foot of a hill, hide for an hour at a chicken farm, walk up half the hill with your helmets on because the rain was like bullets from an Uzi, drink something from a vendor which tasted like rat, flag down a car, beg them to drop you home, give them all your money, almost get hypothermia, reach destination, shower, and drink a couple of bottles of wine and tell everyone about how you dodged death. Now that is a story and no, it doesn't sound like fun (except for the last bit), but that is the memory that sticks out from the entire trip. And to be honest, it was a blast, all things considered.

And that pretty much sums up my take on love. Because I consider myself a fairly realistic person, I know for a fact that it's not going to be unicorns gallping and rainbows throwing up. It's a mix and match of all things good and bad. So once that has been understood, you take the good with the bad and the bad with the good.

As for the pre-requisites, I never had those. I've always considered intelligent, confident men sexier than just the brawny, lobotomized variety. If someone can be smart and hot at the same time, I'd probably chain them to my dining table for good. So aside from that, I would say I steered clear of having any pre-conceived notions about the sort of person I'd like to be with. In short, I tackled my pre-requisite problem with not having any.

Looks, money, fame, and power all have the magical ability to be fleeting. So if you peer too long at them, then you might lose sight of the things that really matter. Looks fade, money comes and goes, fame as we all know does not last forever, and as for power, well, I'd say be powerful in your own right and you won't need to draw from another's.

The beauty in love lies in the fact that it can't be quantified. There is no measure for it. Since it is intangible and without a gauge, you have to rely on your gut. If it feels right, it probably is. If it's not, you then have to learn how to punch yourself in the sternum so that it behaves the next time round.

Acknowledgements

I WANT TO THANK DHRUV FOR ALWAYS BEING THE FIRST person I run to for approval on a thought and also for being my most discerning critic.

Ravina—for going through my work several times without complaining and fixing 'stuff' by sharing her fantastic ideas. Soma and El—for being my most favourite people.

Husain for helping me with statistics and absurd conversation when I most needed it.

Michael for being my rock.

Trisha, my editor, for being so encouraging through the entire process of writing this book.

And all my friends who chipped in with ideas and examples from their lives that I could feed into this book.

A Note on the Author

JUHI PANDE LIVED THE ITINERANT LIFE OF AN AIR FORCE brat for her first two decades; her world consisting of her parents, a dog named Josephine, her brother Dhruv, and a pair of roller skates—in roughly that order. Entertainment comes from the world around you when you grow up on an Air Force base, and so she developed a deep and abiding love of fighter planes, constellations, and other shiny objects, as well as a paralyzing fear of caterpillars.

Juhi moved to Mumbai at the age of 20 to pursue a glamourous career in hotel management, but her dreams were soon crushed and she was subsumed into the humdrum world of music and entertainment television.

She spent eight years working as a television presenter before departing for the thin and somewhat picked over pastures of writing. If she really knows anything about love you probably won't find it in this book, but maybe, just maybe you'll pick up a few useful tips for the journey.

A Note on the Type

SABON IS THE NAME OF AN OLD STYLE SERIF TYPEFACE designed by the German-born typographer and designer Jan Tschichold (1902–74) in the period 1964–7. A distinguishing feature of the typeface was that the roman, italic, and bold weights all occupy the same width when typeset—an unusual feature, but this meant that the typeface then only required one set of copyfitting data (rather than three) when compositors had to estimate the length of a text prior to actual typesetting (a common practice before computer-assisted typesetting).